ATLANTA ARCHITECTURE

Art Deco to Modern Classic, 1929-1959

ATLANTA ARCHITECTURE

Art Deco to Modern Classic, 1929-1959

ROBERT M. CRAIG

Foreword by
RICHARD GUY WILSON

PELICAN PUBLISHING COMPANY
GRETNA 1995

The word "Pelican" and the depiction of a pelican are trademarks
of Pelican Publishing Company, Inc.,
and are registered in the U.S. Patent and Trademark Office.

Library of Congress Cataloging-in-Publication Data

Craig, Robert Michael, 1944-
    Atlanta architecture / Robert Michael Craig ; foreword by Richard Guy
Wilson.
      p. cm.
    Includes bibliographical references and index.
    Contents: Art deco to modern classic, 1929-1959.
    ISBN 0-88289-961-9
    1. Architecture—Georgia—Atlanta. 2. Atlanta (Ga.)—Buildings,
structures, etc. I. Title.
NA735.A83C73 1994
720'.9758'231—dc20   94-2732
                                                   CIP

Manufactured in Hong Kong

Published by Pelican Publishing Company, Inc.
1101 Monroe Street, Gretna, Louisiana 70053

To my parents

Contents

Foreword

SINCLAIR LEWIS OPENED his best-selling novel of 1922, *Babbitt*, with a description that might apply to Atlanta: "the towers of Zenith aspired above the morning mist; austere towers of steel and cement and limestone, sturdy as cliffs and delicate as silver rods . . . The mist took pity on the fretted structures of earlier generations: the Post Office with its shingle-tortured mansard, the red brick minarets of hulking old houses. . . . The city was full of such grotesqueries, but the clean towers were thrusting them from the business center." This could be taken as the credo of many Atlanta businessmen and politicians who in the 1920s transformed the city from a stodgy Victorian into a modern metropolis.

Atlanta was a boomtown—it was founded as one, and it continues to be one—a city on the hustle, whose citizens had no doubt they were the most important city of the region, the "Gate City" of the South. New Orleans might still be a little larger, Birmingham might make steel, but Atlanta was the crossroads, the hub. The consequence for Atlanta in the 1920s was a rivalry as businessmen and city boosters demonstrated their power and success with a magnificent series of towers or skyscrapers, outfitted with lavish ornament and plush lobbies. Showrooms for autos were built in the latest style where the local Babbitts with wives and children could fondle the latest accessories, stroke the smooth fenders, and lust after the latest chrome dream. Another place to fantasize and where dreams seemed to come true was the movie palace, in a building so outrageous with its minarets, parapets, balconies, lobbies, and colored tiles, and with an auditorium where the sun rose and set, and stars twinkled. The observer is still amazed that somebody actually put up the Fox Theatre. Even with the depression of the 1930s there continued to be built in Atlanta remarkable buildings, the crown of which is the Federal Post Office (now the Martin Luther King, Jr. Federal Building) of 1931-33 by Albert Ten Eyck Brown. Anybody who has ever seen this structure with its gleaming granite skin, its piling up of forms and smooth sensuous curves, and the crisp sharply incised ornament recognizes it is a masterpiece, a design worthy of national recognition.

The architecture covered in this book is usually ignored; they are those buildings that do not fit into the canonical stylistic textbooks. One of the reasons is that they are from the recent past, not ancient structures put up by the colonists, or founding fathers. They are not even Victorian, but modern.

Americans can be reverential about their past, even nostalgic for 1930s Fords, but that seldom means action. Indeed in a civilization built from the outset upon disposability, where one can do any damn thing one wants with one's property, buildings are investments; they are replaceable. It is true that in recent years buildings from the 1920s and 1930s that go under the various stylistic names such as Art Deco, Modern Classic, Stripped Classic, Streamlined, PWA, and WPA have received some recognition, but in general we know very little about them.

This volume is one of a very small number of books that examines from a scholarly and critical perspective one of the great periods of American architecture and design, the 1920s and 1930s. It joins similar studies on Fort Worth, Miami, Tulsa, and a very few books that deal with the period in general. Hence it is a pioneering book that records names that are unfamiliar to most of us, figures from the past that even Atlantans might pause at: Albert Ten Eyck Brown, G. Lloyd Preacher, and Pringle and Smith.

This is a book about Atlanta, one of those great American cities that tend to rebuild themselves every forty years or so. Atlanta has history, it has a historical society, but most architectural historians only know Atlanta as where Sherman stopped briefly to burn it, and *Gone with the Wind* was set here. The film opened here as well, not at the Fox, but at Loew's, which had been remodeled into an Art Deco extravaganza by Thomas Lamb of New York. This marvelous palace was torched in 1978 and immediately demolished; the building's bricks were sold as souvenirs. *Sic transit gloria mundi!*

This book by Robert Craig, which is part of a planned multivolume set, is very welcome; it helps clear up a lacuna that exists among most of us about Atlanta. Atlanta, as Craig demonstrates, was no provincial backwater. Its architects, and those individuals who commissioned the buildings, were well aware of the most recent developments in New York, Los Angeles, and Paris. The architects obviously pursued with avidity the latest architectural magazines, the most recent charcoal renderings by Hugh Ferriss, the latest patterns from the Perth Amboy Terra Cotta Works, the latest high-speed elevator from Otis. Atlantans desired to be up-to-date, but that didn't mean that everything had to be new. Most of this book is devoted to commercial and public buildings; only a very few Art Deco houses appear. Most of the businessmen saw the new modern styles as appropriate only for the public or business facade: they lived in stockbroker Tudor, or suburban plantations out in the suburbs

such as Buckhead. This was the other side to Atlanta architecture in these years, a series of period houses done by Neel Reid and Philip Trammell Shutze, whose work has been well documented by other historians. George F. Babbitt and his brethren in Atlanta were adventurers with their commercial property and with public buildings, but when it came to home, tradition ruled. Apparently such disjunctures did not upset Atlantans such as Edward Inman whose major interest lay in racing cars and who held speed records and yet with his wife commissioned the Swan house, that great Baroque-Georgian pile from Shutze in 1926.

This brings up a point to which Craig alludes that is worth keeping in mind. The many terms applied to this architecture—Art Deco, Modern Classic, Depression Modern, Tropical Deco, Streamlined, and others—are really inventions by recent historians. Most of the architects at the time, and the critics who wrote about the new buildings, struggled with the problem of what to call the new architecture. Stylistic terms of that time included: "Modernistic," "Moderne," "Manhattan Style," "vertical style," "cubistic," "jazz," and "International Style." The terms proliferated and an incestuous battle broke out among architects and critics over who most correctly understood the new age. One can spend a great deal of energy trying to define each style—and trying the reader's patience—but one element is crystal clear: all felt a new age had dawned. What that age consisted of would change, but the central feature was the increasing prominence of the machine, as an object, as new technology, as construction, and as a metaphor. The machine had changed life, and it was time that architecture reflected some of these new currents. Atlanta architects responded and created some great buildings.

RICHARD GUY WILSON
University of Virginia

10

Acknowledgments

THIS VOLUME IS THE FIRST to appear of a projected series of studies of the history of Atlanta architecture from the city's founding in 1837 to the present. The author's research on Atlanta architecture began in 1984, was interrupted in 1986-89, and continued happily thereafter with an increased focus on the period under consideration in this volume.

The author wishes to acknowledge, first, the vision of Pelican Publishing Company, which has committed to an extensive and complete visual and written historical record of Atlanta's architecture to be presented in multiple volumes. Frank McGuire at Pelican encouraged the initial proposal.

The author is grateful to Pelican for allowing time both to research necessary new data and to confirm and complete partial building histories earlier recorded in popular and professional publications. Pelican's support has permitted the author to correct misattributions, to establish accurate dates for buildings, and to provide a great deal of new information published here for the first time.

Nina Kooij provided a sharp eye and sound recommendations as editor of this first published volume; the author is grateful for her judicious review at various stages of production.

In spite of the assistance of many individuals during the lengthy period of research and writing of these volumes of *Atlanta Architecture*, the author remains solely responsible for the accuracy of the material published herein. The author welcomes new information that will contribute further to the accuracy and thoroughness of the historical record.

The author gratefully acknowledges the ongoing contributions of Richard Guy Wilson to cultural studies of "the machine age," as author, curator, and teacher, and the author extends his thanks to Professor Wilson for writing the foreword to this volume.

The following architectural firms, institutions, and individuals have been helpful in the process of gathering information in support of this book. The author appreciates the assistance of each, and looks forward to continuing interest in support of future volumes.

The author is indebted to the Atlanta History Center Library and Archives, especially Anne Salter (librarian), Don Rooney (exhibition specialist), and Ted Ryan (curator, photograph collection). The research staff has always been helpful, even five minutes before closing. I especially wish to acknowledge assistance and encouragement, during earlier phases of the Atlanta architectural history project (as defined in 1984), from Nancy Wight and William Richards.

Susan Gwinner of the Atlanta Urban Design Commission has been supportive from the start, providing information on individual buildings as well as assistance with photographic materials.

Joe Patten provided access to the Fox Theatre and continues to be a helpful source of information regarding the history of the theater and its restoration.

Researchers investigating Georgia Tech architecture are particularly indebted to Warren Drury, whose thesis on the early campus development is a fundamental source. David Savini was especially helpful in providing basic data concerning Georgia Tech buildings. Ruth Hale and Joseph Blount of the

Georgia Tech Archives assisted with additional material. Rufus Hughes provided access to the College of Architecture's archive of drawings and photographs of student and alumni projects.

Carol Flores, whose master's thesis and subsequent research substantially increases our knowledge on the subject, was the key source for information on Techwood Homes, Burge and Stevens, and the early work of Stevens and Wilkinson. Tom Ramsey and June Brown of Stevens and Wilkinson clarified certain details regarding the work of Stevens and Wilkinson.

Atlanta historian Franklin Garrett, whose memory is one of the city's cultural resources and whose scholarly publications provide the foundation for much subsequent and ongoing research, was always willing to sort out details regarding buildings of many periods of Atlanta history; he remains a continuing aid to inquiries regarding the history of this city.

Photo processing was by Russell Image Processors Inc. of Atlanta, whose timely accommodation of scheduling requirements was greatly appreciated.

A special acknowledgment is extended to Georgia Tech and Georgia State University students enrolled in recent years in my Atlanta Architecture seminar and whose research projects have contributed in varying ways to this volume: David Eitel, Emilio Etchegoyen, Marty Goldsmith, Jodi Iseman, Barbara Kovaks, Gail Ledbetter, Carole Moore, Carson Pease, Carmen Ponder, and Wendy Taylor.

The support of family is critical to such enterprises, and I am grateful to both Carole and Christopher for the "space" to indulge in my professional love affair with architecture at a time when restoring our Victorian house left very little living space for anyone.

The historical period under consideration in this volume is "on the edge of the historic preservation movement." Buildings fifty years old or older are considered "historic" by preservationists governed by National Register criteria in their surveys of city architecture. In accordance with the limits of its mandate, therefore, the Atlanta Urban Design Commission's historical research through the years has been restricted, for the most part, to the first hundred years of Atlanta's architectural history.

On the other hand, the interest of the local chapter of the American Institute of Architects (AIA) has remained focused more on contemporary design than on historical architectural resources and thus draws more frequent public attention to recent building projects of its own members. The AIA's contribution to the published architectural record has thus been limited to later modern architecture, without support of new historical research, and therefore has added little to the historical record regarding Atlanta's older buildings.

In between these areas of local architectural inquiry falls much of the subject of this and the following volume: buildings too old to be given much attention by the AIA but not old enough to have, for long, been of interest to historians and preservationists. The Deco-to-Modern era is the period of Atlanta's transition from traditional historicism to early modernism, and these essays trace the first phase of that development.

ATLANTA ARCHITECTURE

Art Deco to Modern Classic, 1929-1959

CHAPTER 1

The Four Styles of Modern Architecture

TRADITIONAL V. MODERN SOUTH

The emergence of a modern architecture in Atlanta reflected national and international design trends as the city continued to ignore its provincial location at the foot of the Appalachians, viewing itself instead as the leader of a progressive "New South." A receptivity to modern developments repeatedly set the stage for establishing Atlanta as the premier modern city of the region. Charleston, Savannah, Mobile, and New Orleans, among Southern cities, would retain for generations their respective architectural characters as historic towns formed by Old South values and sustained by traditionalism and a deep sense of family lineage. Such older coastal cities perpetuated antebellum images and a conservative architectural aesthetic, which by the second quarter of the twentieth century was firmly associated with a nostalgic past. The established cities of the Old South valued charm over progressive advances in modern design.

Old Atlanta, during the early twentieth century, reflected a similar traditionalism in its residential architecture of the "academic" tradition, its fine revivalistic houses modeled on Georgian, Neo-Classical, Tudor, Italian Baroque, and American colonial sources. But increasingly, as the city grew and as the twentieth-century urban population was enlarged by a citizenry newly resettled from outside Georgia, the ideal of a New Atlanta competed with traditional forces. Citizens of Atlanta were less and less "native," that is, increasingly not "from" Atlanta. New ideals were imported from New York and from other cultural centers, and a

less provincial outlook characterized a well-traveled, well-educated, and aesthetically less conservative group of architects and clients in Atlanta.

Before World War II, the influence of the new functionalist approach to architectural design (imported from Europe by progressive designers practicing in Southern California and New York) began to be felt in American architectural schools, including Georgia Tech in Atlanta, and in progressive architectural firms. Soon the new modern styles were reflected in built work in developing urban areas throughout the Southeast region: nowhere as extensively as in Miami Beach but also in Shreveport, Louisiana, in Asheville, North Carolina, and with a respectable collection of "Deco-to-Modern" works, as well, in Atlanta. Beginning about 1930 the stirrings of progressive modern design began to alter the architectural character of a changing Deco-era Atlanta and prepared the way in the city for a reception of Bauhaus Modernism following the war.

Among urban centers east of the Mississippi, the city of Atlanta is very young. From the earliest years of American colonial and early national history, the towns of the traditional and essentially rural South were seaboard communities. The spirit of change, from the beginning, looked westward and inland. After the American Revolution, coastal *colonial* capitals in the South (established in towns such as Williamsburg, New Bern, Charleston, and Savannah) moved beyond the "tidewater towns" to establish *state* capitals in counties deeper within the new states—at Richmond, Raleigh, and Columbia, and (by way of Milledgeville, Georgia) at Atlanta. In the case of Atlanta, the city was made capital of Georgia in 1879, merely forty-two years after the city's founding in 1837.

Thus Atlanta, about the same age as Chicago, was already a new town, 200 years younger than such colonial capitals as Boston; Atlanta is a city which developed entirely in the late nineteenth and twentieth centuries. In the upper Midwest, the contemporary, Victorian-era, new city of Chicago rapidly developed a progressive "Western" school of modern architecture, skyscraper design, and engineering innovation led by Louis Sullivan and (Georgia-born) John Root. Chicago established a reputation for progressive design which no American city matched, inventing the skyscraper as the new building type by which any city's modern image and economic development might be gauged. During Atlanta's first skyscraper age, at the turn of the twentieth century, only one city competed with the Georgia capital as the leader of an emerging New South, and that was the steel-financed urban center of Birmingham, Alabama.

Birmingham's early skyscrapers, from the turn of the century to the 1920s, rivaled Atlanta's as translations of a new commercial style and modern building type, and the pioneer skyscrapers in both cities reflected their competition for leadership in the central South. Birmingham was the steel city of the region, the "Pittsburgh of the South," and the modern skyscraper was framed in steel. But Atlanta was historically at the transportation crossroads of the South, a fact made dramatically evident earlier in the city's history when Gen. William Tecumseh Sherman burned the city and destroyed its railroad during the Civil War. As Atlanta urban historians have demonstrated, key transportation developments (maintaining Atlanta as a crossroads for rail, interstate highway, and finally air transportation) ensured that the city would leave Birmingham and other emerging urban areas behind in the race for primacy in the New South.[1]

It would be the more progressive leaders of Southern cities such as Atlanta that later would be receptive to the fresh architectural images of Art Deco (applied in the late 1920s in Atlanta to a second period of skyscraper construction), to the Streamlined Moderne, and to the Modern. The fashionable modernism of Art Deco, spreading from Paris and New York from the mid-1920s on, would gain a rapid popularity as it was applied to the facades of commercial buildings nationwide. Within a decade or so, Art Deco would effect an urban face-lift to Main Streets throughout the country, including the South.

Most certainly, Miami Beach, Florida, is unique from any perspective as the nation's most extensive repository of "Deco delights."[2] Deco-era South Miami Beach offers a unique case of a new town of the period built on virtually virgin soil. Stimulated by a pioneer spirit of real-estate entrepreneurial development and fueling a 1920s land boom in South Florida, builders turned to progressive architects and designers for a distinctively modern resort aesthetic. South Miami Beach's extraordinary "Art Deco" district of small hotels, apartment buildings, and commercial buildings of Modernistic, Moderne, and "Tropical Deco"[3] styles is unsurpassed in this country, perhaps in the world. As an emerging center for progressive architecture in the South, Miami Beach inaugurated the birth of the Sun-Belt South—resort oriented and linked to recreation, to tourist and retirement accommodations, and to commerce. As a new city, lacking the traditional roots of an Old South community, Miami Beach developed at the moment modern styles were first introducing progressive architectural images onto the national scene.

Atlanta's "Deco-to-Modern" era both compares and contrasts with such developments. Atlanta was neither a completely new seedbed for Modernistic germination, as was Miami Beach, nor was it a long-established community like Charleston or Mobile, culturally entrenched in Old South traditions. A city of mid-nineteenth-century foundation, Atlanta was not yet a century old by the Deco era and had not established deep enough roots to resist modernism as effectively as might the historic communities of the Old South. Moreover, Atlanta developed the economic opportunity, population, transportation, and commercial enterprise that promoted its prosperity; its office buildings, industrial and transportation structures, and commercial centers emerged in modern form as the city grew.

Art Deco and avant-garde Modern were not images typically associated with the traditional, agrarian South; progressive architecture was urban and not rural, while the Old South remained even in the mid-twentieth century distinctly rural with farms and small towns. Thus, historic forces were already ranged against a wide receptivity of modern architecture in the region, although isolated urban areas show exceptional progressive strains. In the end, it would be in those emerging new cities of the New South that a modern aesthetic would be especially assertive, and eventually "progressive" small towns, seeking to modernize their downtowns in emulation of big-city business district streetscapes, would display a competitive up-to-datedness in new facades for commercial main streets. By 1930, Atlanta had the largest population of any city in the South except New Orleans, and Atlanta topped a list of eighteen Southeastern cities (from St. Louis to Miami and Richmond to Houston) in issuing the most building permits of any urban area in the region.[4] The stage was set for the Deco-to-Modern era.

The architectural reflection of this rise of modern Atlanta is neither isolated from national and international currents nor monolithic in its expression. There is no singular "modern" architecture during the era "from Deco to early Modern," nor is Atlanta's progressive architecture regionally unique and distinctive as an ensemble, as clearly can be said of Miami Beach Deco. Atlanta's modern styles are, first, reflections locally of emerging national images for new skyscrapers and commercial chain stores, for modern governmental buildings, and for roadside architecture. After the Second

World War, local architects took the lead in introducing a more avant-garde image and adapting it to housing projects, schools, hospitals, and small professional buildings.

Four distinct styles can be identified as progressive architectural currents of the period from the late twenties to the post-World-War-II era. Each is "modern" but varies in its reflection of aesthetic tendencies generally associated with modernism: abstraction, simplicity, a-historicism, a technological or mechanistic aesthetic, progressivism. In spite of shared elements and a common spirit of contemporaneity, the four phases of modern architecture derive from separate sources and reflect different influences; each presents distinctive formal images, employs decoration in varied ways (or eschews it), and reflects the work of different designers—often different *types* of designers.

Each of the four "styles" of modern building, therefore, remains unique and identifiable. While hybrids are the more normal expressions of Deco-era modernism, as local designers interpret the new styles to their own purposes, the four distinctive expressions retain identities as separate manifestations of a new aesthetic age. The modern styles of Atlanta architecture between the late 1920s and the late 1950s we may call Art Deco, Modern Classic, Streamlined Moderne, and Modern.

The first two, evident from the late 1920s through the 1930s, are treated in this volume. They share a more conservative approach to modern design in finding ornamental sources in nature and in historic architectural languages, specificaly classicism. The last two, treated in the following volume, are more directly linked to the machine and translate their borrowings from the machine more abstractly, thus appearing more modern.

Art Deco and Modern Classic design may be viewed as an effort of traditional, often Beaux-Arts-trained architects to be progressive. The Streamlined Moderne and Modern, however, looked to industrial design, a factory aesthetic, and technology for artistic impulses achieved through streamlining in the first instance and through a progressive

AT RIGHT: *Southern Bell Telephone Company Building, Marye, Alger, and Vinour, 1929 (photo from Robert M. Craig Collection, Atlanta History Center)*

abstraction in the second. Discarding historic form altogether was something the first two were not always prepared to do, as Mayan-derived ornament in Deco buildings and the New Deal classicism of Modern Classic demonstrated. The more progressive Streamlined Moderne and Modern looked to ships, airplanes, trains, and automobiles for inspiration; they expressed speed in movement, economy of line, and a modern functionalist efficiency above all. Thus, while it can be argued that the Deco-to-Modern era offers continuities of progressive design, the cosmetic, more conservative, and still historicist examples of Deco-era Atlanta architecture are treated in this volume and the more abstract, machine aesthetic of late-1930s Streamlined Moderne and 1940s and early 1950s Modern are treated in the following volume. Historians continue to debate whether these aesthetic manifestations are four phases of Deco architecture, four distinct styles, or four dimensions of modernism in American design. Beyond what they share as reflections of the Machine Age, we may identify their distinctive characteristics as follows.

ART DECO

"Art Deco" stylisms were the earliest evidence of a designer's self-conscious effort to present a modern style, and "Deco" was manifested in forms of all sizes, from jewelry to architecture. As the term "Art Deco" implies, it is essentially a *decorative art* aesthetic; that is, it was especially popular in its decorative arts forms: furniture, jewelry, fashion, and interior design. And as an architectural aesthetic, it was essentially ornamental. Its glamor and sense of style were found in its color and exoticism. Deco delighted itself in coloristic patterns, jazzy zigzag lines and profiles, and syncopated rhythms of tapestry surfaces, repeat borders, and variegated accents. The Deco designer was essentially an ornamentalist who subscribed to John Ruskin's nineteenth-century view of architecture as ornamented construction.[5]

The Deco style was often cosmetic and

could be theatrical, and it found its architectural expression on buildings associated with these enterprises: boutiques, novelty shops and five and dimes, theaters, and commercial buildings. The basic building forms were often traditional, economic retail boxes whose facades were cosmetically "dolled up" with Deco face-lifts. Polychromatic terra-cotta, patterned brickwork, Vitrolite, and glass block added color, light reflection, sheen, and polish to the marketplace, and Art Deco ornament brought a populist form of modern architecture to the city during the prosperous late 1920s.

In addition to its essential nature as a style of design, the very *term* "Art Deco" derives from decorative arts, most especially from the 1925 Paris show, L'Exposition Internationale des Arts Décoratifs et Industriels Modernes. "Arts Décoratifs" became "Art Deco," and as the most pluralistic of the four modern aesthetics, its sources were widespread. Scholars have found roots in the early Prairie work of Frank Lloyd Wright, the abstract patterns of the Viennese Secession Movement in Austria, Picasso's and Braque's Cubism, the architect Dudok's work in Holland, and pre-Columbian decoration of

Mesoamerica, which might be Aztec or Toltec but was generalized in its 1920s revived forms as "Mayan Revival."

Nature might be transformed into a simplified "modern" configuration: in a decorative motif by Wright, for instance, of a hollyhock in a leaded window, or in a sculptural carving or foliate pattern carved by a Mayan craftsman, rediscovered in a pre-Columbian monument. In both such transformations, a flower was abstracted as it was reinterpreted by a twentieth-century Deco artist. Deco designers stenciled, faceted, or standardized for pattern use numerous natural forms, now modernized for machine-cut translation on an Art Deco building panel or decorative frieze. The result, in cut stone or terra-cotta, on a stencil border, mural frame, or stained glass, was sensual and colorful. Considered both chic and progressive, Art Deco proffered a sense of the "latest fashion" in design. Deco delighted the eye, appealed more to the emotions than to the intellect, and became universally popular by the late 1920s. In so doing, it became the people's style of modernism.

MODERN CLASSIC

By the early 1930s the optimism, prosperity, and ebullience of the Roaring Twenties had been shocked by the Great Crash and displaced by the realities and economies of the depression. Decoration and cosmetics were now considered architecturally superfluous and unaffordable, and restraint became a watchword of the day. Regardless of its recurrent revivalism and its associations with an established "academic" traditionalism, classicism could offer 1930s architects, nevertheless, a "new" simplicity and economic means for achieving a basic sense of style in architectural design.

Since much of the decade's construction was government sponsored, the "authority" of classicism appropriately informed government architecture. Indeed, federal buildings were already reflecting such restrained Modern Classic tendencies during the Hoover years.[6] But the image is especially

Federal Post Office Building, A. Ten Eyck Brown (Alfredo Barili, Jr., and J. W. Humphreys, associates; James Wetmore, supervising architect), 1931-33 (photo by Robert M. Craig)

associated with the depression years and with New Deal architecture. Within the first "hundred days" of the inauguration of Franklin Delano Roosevelt as president, the federal government established the Public Works Administration (PWA) to sponsor building projects across the country. The Works Progress Administration (WPA), established in May 1935, was more directly an employment bill and was intended to return thousands of unemployed to the work force. The quintessential modern bureaucratic style of architecture during the thirties became a PWA/WPA Modern Classic, sometimes referred to as "Depression Modern."[7] Both the PWA and WPA financed building projects in Atlanta during the 1930s and early 1940s.

The essential historic root of the Modern Classic style is, self-evidently, classicism, but the immediate influence came from Beaux-Arts-trained Philadelphia architect and teacher Paul Philippe Cret, who reinterpreted and adapted ancient forms to modern purpose. The contemporary classical expression during the 1930s was a classicism marked by modern restraint, by economies of line and form, and by a reductiveness distinctly reflective of the years of depression. Simple, finely detailed, and well-proportioned forms bred a monumentality immediately adopted for government projects.

19

The designers of the Modern Classic were not the ornamental stylists and fashion-conscious creators of Art Deco, but official architects, or local designers given work by an increasingly vast bureaucracy.

This was federal architecture in spirit and often in reality, and it found its national expression in federal post offices, war memorials, federal office buildings, county courthouses, and civic centers, including police stations, city halls, and courts buildings. Its stylistic forms found their way into school designs sponsored by the PWA. Throughout the thirties commercial architecture also manifested features of the bureaucratic "Depression Modern," formed as a simplified Beaux-Arts Classical style and embodying a minimalist traditionalism. A shopping center or commercial building could reflect the spirit of both a restrained classicism and contemporary modernism without adding the self-indulgent ornamental colorism of the now passé polychromatic Deco. The Modern Classic established itself during the 1930s as a traditionalist modern style of the New Deal era.

STREAMLINED MODERNE

Although the Streamlined Moderne and Modern are treated in the following volume, a word or two contrasting them with Art Deco and Modern Classic is in order here. Both streamlining and the new materials, processes, and technologies of modernity reflected the spirit of efficiency and economy that characterized the 1930s and post-Second World War years. Both Streamlined Moderne and Modern stripped away the decorative surface treatments of Art Deco and the historical references of the Modern Classic, and they expressed in abstract form the new age of "space/time." Plainer and planar walls, flowing lines, continuous spaces, volumetric abstractions, and dematerialized transparencies reflected both a "nonrepresentational" abstraction that paralleled modern art and a space/time relativity that paralleled modern science.

The Modern style was as abstract and advanced as Picasso and Einstein. Modern was

the progressive style. It avoided formal texture, color, and ornament, and it often left the general public behind, remaining intellectual and elitist at the very moment it declared itself international and universal. Unlike Art Deco, Modern remained out of the mainstream of popular culture (although Streamlined Moderne may arguably be regarded the machine aesthete's populist style); it would require a Post-Modern revival of the roadside streamlined aesthetic and the Neo-Deco of the late 1980s and 1990s to bring the general public around again as they embrace the Neo-Modernistic of recent years. Because the term "Moderne" was employed generally in the 1920s and 1930s to refer to various progressive styles, especially what we here call Art Deco, it remains necessary to define our own concept of Streamlined Moderne as a distinct expression of the progressive age.

Throughout the twenties and thirties, Americans had developed a love affair with the most progressive and liberating "machine" of the modern age: the automobile. In 1925 there were 20 million automobiles in the United States, and by 1940 there were 42 million. The forms of this machine had changed dramatically from the "horseless

carriage" era of the Model T (manufactured between 1908 and 1927) and the Model A (which first appeared in 1927) to the streamlined classic "coupes" of the 1930s. Raymond Loewy's 1934 Hupmobile (designed 1932), the Chrysler Air Flow (1934), the Lincoln Zephyr (1936), and the Cord 810 (1936) established a new standard for automobile design, and the essential determinant of this new spirit was streamlining.

The effects of streamlining touched every aspect of American design—from decorative arts to industrial design, from transportation machines to architecture. A new design professional emerged in the industrial designer, and by the late 1930s streamlining was becoming established as the central motif of the third phase of modern architecture, the Streamlined Moderne. The aesthetic is marked especially by the "lines of speed"—the parallel horizontal bands that gave expression to the dynamic movement of new streamlined trains, cars, and buses. The curved corners, molded profiles, and kinetics of flowing tear-drop shapes soon transformed blocky, cubic, and angular forms of an earlier machine aesthetic to the economies and dynamic "lines of least resistance" of a new age.[8]

The industrial designer applied principles of streamlining to instruments and machines from fountain pens and telephones to ocean liners and automobiles. With its emphasis on movement, streamlining was especially suitable to transportation design and to roadside architecture. Industrial designer Norman Bel Geddes, who published a series of progressive designs in 1932 in his book *Horizons*, by the end of the decade would play a leading role in designing the 1939 New York World's Fair, "The World of Tomorrow."[9] In *Horizons*, Bel Geddes's streamlined ocean liner, super-scaled "aeroplane," and "house of the future," as well as contemporary train and car designs by Raymond Loewy, established models for streamlined forms that architects soon adapted to a "Streamlined Moderne" style of building, especially to buildings associated with transportation machines themselves. These structures included bus depots, marine casinos, dockside restaurants, beach pavilions, air terminals, and various automobile buildings from gas stations and roadside diners to auto-parts stores, garages, and car dealerships. Streamlined Moderne became America's third phase of modern architecture, and it was especially popular in the late 1930s and 1940s.[10]

MODERN

Of the four phases of modern architecture, it is the fourth to which the specific stylistic term "Modern" (with a capital *M*) applies. It is the final reflection of a gradual abstraction in architecture marked by both a complete independence from historic precedent (although its structural rationalism derives from classicism) and (in its purest form) a rejection of color and ornament, those very decorative elements that had been the mainstay of Art Deco. Thus, progressive design had reversed itself. The machine-cut ornament and coloristic appliqué of Art Deco had given place to a fourth phase of modernism, a Modern architecture of distinctly different features.

Characteristics of the Modern style included steel and concrete frame construction (including pipe columns and pipe railings bounding flat roofs, balconies, and terraces), glass enclosures (giving Modern buildings a volumetric rather than massive formal character), and planar surfaces (devoid of both

Price Gilbert, Jr., House, Burge and Stevens (James Wilkinson, designer), 1939 (remodeled, Stevens and Wilkinson, 1964); razed (photo courtesy of Stevens and Wilkinson)

Deco incisions and colorful in-set panels, PWA classical friezes and pilasters, and streamlined streaks and curved corners). The Modern aesthetic found beauty in functionalism—the ability of the building to serve directly its intended purposes.

Modern architectural forms essentially derive from the factory aesthetic and architectural abstractions that Walter Gropius and his colleagues had developed at the Bauhaus school in Germany during the mid-1920s, and which they applied especially to housing projects. Le Corbusier in France, J. J. P. Oud in Holland, and other Europeans evolved a similar purist Modern aesthetic, which together with German developments was recognized as an "International Style" of European Modernism.[11]

It is with reference to this European Modern architectural avant-garde—the Bauhaus aesthetic and International Style—that the fourth style of Atlanta modernism may be simply called Modern. It is neither Art Deco, Modern Classic, nor Streamlined Moderne, but it shares with each an effort to be contemporary, progressive, and free of academic historicism. As Tom Wolfe has noted, Modern architecture was brought "from Bauhaus to our house," and its essential reflection in Atlanta is associated with the shift at Georgia Institute of Technology's School of Architecture from the Beaux-Arts Classical tradition in architectural education to an increasing interest in functionalism as a design determinant. Thus, as this volume demonstrates, Art Deco and Modern Classic are rooted in Beaux-Arts academic traditions. Streamlined Moderne and Modern are rooted in the machine, in functionalism, and (in the case of Modern) in the Bauhaus.

FOUR STYLES
OF MODERN ARCHITECTURE

The definition of four discrete phases of modern architecture—Art Deco, Modern Classic, Streamlined Moderne, and Modern—serves to organize the consideration of the progressive architecture of Atlanta from the late 1920s through the 1950s in this and the following volume. The concept of "style" merely attempts to group buildings (or other objects) into categories of shared elements, features in common, much like identifying species in the worlds of botany or ornithology. Sometimes the shared elements result from common design sources, and thus an understanding of the models that inspired architects in their forming of new works helps to clarify both the similarities and differences among the respective groups of buildings.

Some architects especially excelled in one of the four aesthetics or worked exclusively or predominantly in that one style. Moreover, each of the styles is associated with certain building types more than with others, and there are chronological differences in the development of each aesthetic that further isolate the four modern styles from one another. In embracing varying progressive images of design for its buildings, Atlanta reflected the national (even international) character of a twenties-to-fifties modernism, which is not homogeneous.

Moreover, these four phases of modern American architecture were frequently evidenced, across the country, in crossbred rather than pure stylistic form. Modern architectural hybrids were not only frequent but typical as local architects began to respond to changing national developments. Early depression-era courthouses, post offices, and war memorials formed in the Modern Classic often continued to employ minimal incised ornamentation in the Art Deco tradition of a few years earlier. Similarly, a 1940s Modern professional building reflecting the "International Style" aesthetic might also employ the horizontal "lines of speed" and curved entries or streamlined building corners echoing the Moderne.

Thus, one should not be surprised that many Atlanta examples of modern architecture evidence stylistic overlap, reflecting influence from the varied progressive currents of the day. Many local modern buildings lacked the theoretical conviction or critical urgency to embody the intellectual "purism" of a more canonical European Modern. Others applied formal or decorative features from one phase of modern design onto another. Despite their divergent aesthetics, designers of works in any of the four styles declared their projects to be modern and progressive. Yet in Atlanta, the Art Deco of Pringle and Smith, the Streamlined Moderne of George Bond, the Modern Classic of Ivey and Crook or A. Ten Eyck Brown, and the Modern of Bush-Brown, Gailey, and Heffernan or Stevens and Wilkinson differ from one another almost as much as all four differ from academic, Beaux-Arts architecture, and, in so doing, each declares itself to be modern. The era of Atlanta architecture—from Art Deco to Modern—reflects national currents but presents itself, as well, as a unique expression of the development of modern architecture in the New South.

Light, City Hall, G. Lloyd Preacher, 1929-30 (photo by Robert M. Craig)

FAR RIGHT: Light, W. W. Orr Building, Pringle and Smith, 1930 (photo by Robert M. Craig)

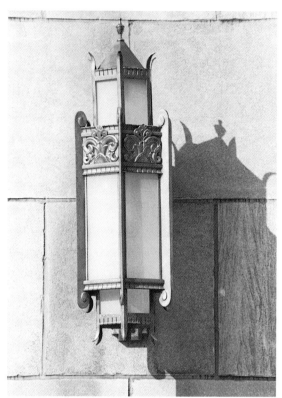

Neon, marquee, Plaza Theater, Briarcliff Shopping Plaza, George Harwell Bond, 1939 (photo by Robert M. Craig, courtesy of Atlanta Urban Design Commission)

FAR RIGHT: Light, J. C. Murphy High School, Barili and Humphreys, 1947-49 (photo by Robert M. Craig)

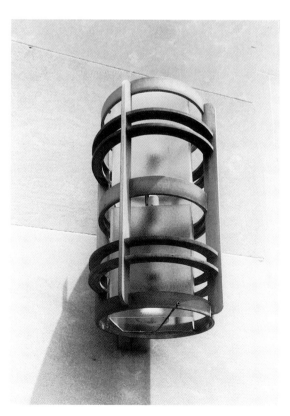

CHAPTER 2

Art Deco: Ornamented Construction as Facade Cosmetic

It is demonstrable that basic to the development and acceptance of the Moderne
was the existence of, and regard for, democratic, egalitarian, middle-class, commercial,
free-enterprise, popular culture values and comprehensions.

FORREST F. LISLE, 1972

It is not by accident that the facade gives the momentary impression of being a back-drop . . .
that the architects believe a facade can be more successfully painted . . .
on a building than modelled on one.

HAROLD R. SHURTLEFF, 1927

. . . merely another way of decorating surfaces.

ALFRED H. BARR, 1932

AMONG THE FOUR STYLES of early modern architecture in America, Art Deco was the earliest, the most colorful, and the most widely popular. It spread its ornamental patterns around entry doors of office buildings, it crowned skyscrapers with decorative bands and foliate panels, and it provided cosmetic face-lifts to facades of Main Street stores from metropolis to small town. Its renewed use of terra-cotta and its machine-cut floral and figural reliefs introduced a new decorative richness that became the hallmark of the end of the Roaring Twenties.

Moreover, its new materials literally made over the face of America. Formica covered interior walls and was found on counter tops in cafés or home kitchens under Bakelite radios, colorful Plaskon, and Beetleware. Monel Metal, a copper and nickel alloy, trimmed soda-fountain surfaces and diner interiors, while stainless steel and aluminum adorned streamlined architecture like chrome-accented automobiles. And Vitrolite appeared in hotels,

restaurants, and theaters and masked traditional storefronts nationwide, hiding those "Main Street" historical faces of molded brick, cast iron, or stone which a younger generation now thought showed the aging lines of past eras (see colorplate, p. 96). With slick images of a new modernism, Art Deco architecture in movie theaters, boutiques, or jazzed-up office lobbies presented a colorful and rhythmic ornamentalism, an *art décoratif* that found widespread expression in jewelry design, furniture, and the boutiques and department stores that sold them.

Indeed, department stores joined metropolitan hotels and theaters as the "people's palaces" of the Deco Era.[1] Their architects composed, along urban streets, Jazz-Age profiles, building setbacks, and dramatic towers. A new breed of stylish designers adorned building facades and feather-crowned skyscraper rooflines with the new cosmetic of Deco. If the depression years influenced simpler lines and restraint, the mid-thirties department store still often

*William-Oliver Building,
Pringle and Smith, 1930
(photo by Robert M. Craig)*

evidenced setback profiles, decorative panels between window levels, and an emphasis on facade as cosmetic.

Late-twenties Americans viewed Art Deco as progressive and fashionable yet traditional. The public was accustomed to an eclectic architecture of formal mass, surface adornment, and beauty—a beauty considered to be the product of the "art" of architecture. In the tradition of John Ruskin, architecture was the "fine art" of building, that is, construction ornamented. Ruskin's definition of architecture embraced the view that architecture was the art of constructing an edifice which meets its occupant's practical requirements but which also "impresses on its form certain character, venerable or beautiful, but otherwise unnecessary."[2] An ornamental modernism, Art Deco architecture served the demand for beauty by a public not yet prepared to accept the intellectual abstractions and colorless functionalism of naked Modern engineering. By contrast, this late phase of functionalist Modern, an aesthetic less popular than Art Deco, would declare beauty to be inherent in the efficiency of a structure of economic lines and surfaces. The fourth style of modern architecture

revered the science of building. Art Deco, on the other hand, promoted the art of decorating building.

Art Deco's popular appeal was a product of its self-evident display of the art, rather than the science, of building. Deco was an

FAR RIGHT: *Regenstein's,
Pringle and Smith, 1929-30 (photo from Robert M. Craig Collection, Atlanta History Center)*

art of sensual colorism, of decorative patterns, and of references to traditional ornamental forms—flowers, human figures, even stylized classical volutes—however abstracted they may appear in Deco friezes and incised panels. Although expressed in progressive, apparently machine-cut forms, Deco floral patterns and faceted figural reliefs remained recognizably linked to nature and to known forms, unlike International Style Modern, which abjured ornament altogether. In linear patterns, palm leaves, friezes of flowers in blossom, and bird and human profiles surfaced late-twenties buildings with the new ornament.

Art Deco's repeat-patterned modernism, suggesting stencil, die, or stamp application, was, nevertheless, aesthetically less mechanistic than the transportation-oriented forms of the Streamlined Moderne. And it was stylish and emotionally evocative more than it was intellectual, in contrast with the functionalist aesthetic of the Modern. Moreover, its employment of historic architectural languages, in referencing Mayan or American Indian patterns, remained more exotic and colorful than the more restrained classicism of the "PWA" Modern Classic. Deco, therefore, is both like and unlike the three other phases of modern design. Despite the numerous hybrids and the shared spirit among modern styles, Art Deco remains identifiable and unique; it offers peculiar ornamental features, distinct aesthetic roots, and a sense of style particularly its own.

In Atlanta, an emerging interest in surface pattern and color juxtaposition was already apparent in the 1910s in brick buildings accented with stone or terra-cotta trim. Two such works by major Atlanta architects have recently been demolished. The "New" North Exchange Building for Southern Bell Telephone Company, built in 1916 by P. Thornton Marye, included ornate terra-cotta trim around window and door openings and at parapet level against cream brick walls. A similar richness of surface was achieved by the dark brick employed by A. Ten Eyck Brown at the 1914 YMCA Building. Strongly contrasting stone keystones

and stringcourse—patterned across a rich brick field—created a distinctive and urbane structure that was regrettably demolished as recently as 1991 for a parking lot.

The YMCA Building's architect, A. Ten Eyck Brown, was the leading figure in Atlanta's transition from historic eclecticism toward Art Deco during the early and mid-1920s. Willing to work in a monumental Beaux-Arts Classical style, Brown also oversaw an early interest among city architects in Near Eastern ornament and color extending from Byzantine and Romanesque to Islamic forms. Surface patterns of brickwork and terra-cotta historically had colored Byzantine and ancient Near Eastern architecture, and they found their way to Atlanta in the early-1920s schools constructed under the general purview of A. Ten Eyck Brown as supervising architect.

The best were Edwards and Sayward's 1924 Girls' High School (later Roosevelt High, and recently converted to residential use as The Roosevelt) and Booker T. Washington High School (1922-24) designed by Eugene C. Wachendorff. Washington High, Atlanta's first public high school for blacks, presented a brick veneer over reinforced concrete frame and was enriched with diaper patterns over its main Romanesque arches and below a crowning cornice of corbeled brick. Decorative accents especially gave focus to the main entry.[3]

YMCA, A. Ten Eyck Brown, 1913-14 (photo from Robert M. Craig Collection, Atlanta History Center)

27

Booker T. Washington High School, Eugene C. Wachendorff, 1922-24 (photo by Robert M. Craig)

brickwork, inset stones, carved arches, and foliate friezes, which gives the building a surface interest that sets the stage for Deco pattern-making later in the same decade.

A. Ten Eyck Brown continued to edge Atlanta toward Deco ornamentalism as his work of the early decade reflected and further encouraged a receptivity to color and to a modulation of historic forms of architecture. Brown's 1920 United Motors Service Building (see colorplate) stands today in a section of Peachtree Street once considered an "automobile row" because of the concentration of auto dealerships and service facilities located there. The south elevation displays the building's utilitarian function, but Brown delighted in presenting displays of patterned brickwork along the west (Peachtree Street) and south elevations. The colossal colonnade of the west front is set *in antis*—that is, within framing walls—and establishes five monumental bays of windows, the whole outlined in a colorful terra-cotta border of Greek frets. Brown created here a grand stoa for automobiles, linked to ancient Hellenistic mercantile buildings which flanked the agora or marketplace, but looking forward, in its interest in color, to Art

While Washington High's brickwork reflected the interest in ornament characteristic of the prosperous twenties, Roosevelt High (see colorplate) looked to a specific historical precedent for its entry detail, the lion porch of S. Zeno Maggiore in Verona. Moreover, Roosevelt crowns the whole school building block with a Byzantine-inspired dome. But it is Roosevelt's material richness, its surface patterns combining tapestry

Roosevelt High School (formerly Girls' High School, now The Roosevelt), Edwards and Sayward (A. Ten Eyck Brown, supervising architect), 1924 (photo by Robert M. Craig)

Deco ornamentalism. Its various decorative features and historic references lend a dignity to this utilitarian building that serves to ennoble the automobile at the moment "the machine" was capturing the imagination of Atlantans and Americans generally.

A series of skyscraper projects at the end of the decade recounts Atlanta's final shift from historicism to Deco stylisms. The leading architects of the period to participate in Atlanta's Deco styling—Pringle and Smith, P. Thornton Marye, and G. Lloyd Preacher—had all worked under Brown's supervision on 1920s public schools.[4] Pringle and Smith's Rhodes-Haverty Building (1929) echoed Lombardic Romanesque corbeling (see colorplate) popularized in several of Atlanta's schools of the period—Preacher's Whitefoord Elementary (1928-29) or Pringle and Smith's more elaborate Joseph E. Brown West Junior High (1923-24). Atlanta's tallest building for a quarter of a century, the Rhodes-Haverty lifted its historicist terracotta arcade twenty-one stories to the sky, where its colorful tiara crowned the downtown skyline at a height just surpassing the city's tallest structure since 1906, the Candler Building.

Ever since Chicago skyscraper innovator Louis Sullivan likened the tall building to a classical column, skyscraper designers have composed these vertical urban landmarks in three sections: a base (the building's entry and mezzanine), a column shaft (the stacked office units), and a capital (the skyscraper's crowning cornice, sometimes with mechanical equipment within). At the Rhodes-Haverty Building, the decorative "capital" is

edged in Romanesque corbeled arches. Its slightly projecting gable capping rounded arched windows reinforces the varied treatment of the innermost four windows and was defined by a more prominent setback in the original design. This bay, which originally related more to the ground-level entry, helped to unite the three elements of the vertical office shaft, providing the frontispiece for the traditionally rooted composition. Panels in lighter color appear to form horizontal bands behind the continuous vertical shafts, whose narrow width and vertical elongation bring an expression of skyward aspiration to the facade, much as Sullivan had done in pioneer skyscrapers of the 1890s.

With the Rhodes-Haverty Building, Pringle and Smith announced a new scale for urban Atlanta. The Rhodes-Haverty would remain the city's tallest skyscraper until the 1954 erection of the Fulton National Bank Building, a work of the fourth, or Modern, phase of Atlanta's progressive architecture. But skyscrapers in the early 1920s had emerged in more conservative dress. With the Haas-Howell Building of 1922, the Glenn, McGlawn Bowen, and Bona Allen buildings of 1923, and the Carnegie Building of 1926, downtown Atlanta experienced a surge of new office construction, although the generally restrained style and detailing of these earlier works were rooted in traditional

rather than modern sources. At the end of the decade, Atlanta was again starting to build skyscrapers and both exterior and interior walls would be surfaced with a progressive ornamental styling. Combining both Lombardic Romanesque and proto-Deco ornamental detail, the Rhodes-Haverty Building presents itself as a transition from a colorful historicism to a colorful progressivism.

In the architects' original design for the Rhodes-Haverty Building, the top three floors were to be set back at each corner, echoing the "Modernistic" tendency toward setback profiles and ziggurat towers of the era. The gabled arcades were originally to be capped by a pyramidal roof and cupola, later eliminated, and the entire building was to be faced in granite with terra-cotta trim. Although constructed with brick facing, the 1929 structure retained its decorative treatment, including ornate two-story storefronts of metal and plate glass, regrettably obliterated a generation ago by the granite veneer of the 1967 Brooks Brothers remodeling of the ground-floor and mezzanine-level facade.

In the fall of 1928, Atlanta's Chamber of Commerce monthly magazine, *The City Builder*, quoted the architects' description of the building as "of distinct American design . . . an unusually handsome landmark . . . the very latest word in office building, and the first of its kind in the South." James Joseph Haverty, whose investment company constructed the building, remarked that "beauty should be combined with utility, 'thereby developing standards of culture in architecture which will represent the energy, imagination, and aspirations of the American spirit.'" He considered that inasmuch as "Atlanta is looked upon as the center of the culture of the South," then "in this new building is to be illustrated that spirit of culture which belongs to the South."[5] In setting the stage for an emerging, progressive beauty in skyscraper architecture, an *art décoratif* that combined beauty and utility for a New South urban building type, Pringle and Smith's Rhodes-Haverty Building was significant as a proto-Deco landmark.

Detail, architect's presentation drawing, Rhodes-Haverty Building, Pringle and Smith, 1929 (base subsequently resurfaced by Brooks Brothers) (photo by Robert M. Craig, courtesy of Henry Howard Smith, Architect)

Pringle and Smith soon established themselves as Atlanta's premier Art Deco firm. The architects immediately turned their attention to a prime site at the "Five Points" intersection of Peachtree and Marietta streets where in 1929-30 they erected the sixteen-story William-Oliver Building, Atlanta's first completed Art Deco skyscraper. Developed by the Healey Real Estate and Improvement Company and named for William T. Healey, Jr., and Oliver M. Healey, the office building faced its steel frame with ashlar and then surfaced its flat facade with Art Deco incisions and ornamental moldings. The zigzag frieze, comparatively isolated on the Rhodes-Haverty Building, is now interlaced among floral patterns in an elaborate network of Deco elements. The band presents a parade of splayed, broad-leafed tropical plants (abstracted yuccas or lily leaves), which recall classical Ionic volutes. Throughout, a jazzy syncopation of chevrons in echelon (and elsewhere the continuous flow of wave motifs)

ABOVE AND AT LEFT: *Mezzanine ornaments, William-Oliver Building, Pringle and Smith, 1930 (photos by Robert M. Craig)*

FAR LEFT: *William-Oliver Building, Pringle and Smith, 1930 (photo by Robert M. Craig)*

BELOW: *Decorative frieze, William-Oliver Building, Pringle and Smith, 1930 (photo by Robert M. Craig)*

ABOVE: *Regenstein's, Pringle and Smith, 1929-30 (photo from Robert M. Craig Collection, Atlanta History Center)*

BELOW: *Peters Land Company insignia, Regenstein's, Pringle and Smith, 1929-30 (photo from Robert M. Craig Collection, Atlanta History Center)*

serves to ornament friezes at various levels of a spirited Deco facade. Marblework and bronze grills in the lobby display a similar richness achieved through fine materials and patterned decorations (see colorplates).

Two other period buildings by Pringle and Smith mark the move northward from the central business district of turn-of-the-century "downtown" to a new "uptown." The first site is a location that in the 1930s would become a significant commercial district and that in the 1960s and 1970s would emerge as a convention hotel district developed by John Portman and called Peachtree Center. In 1929-30 the Peters Land Company built a store at 209 Peachtree on the site of the 1903 First Baptist Church.[6] The new store was decorated with full-fledged Deco ornament (including an interlace of *P*, *L*, and *Co*) between windows of the top floor. First occupied by Regenstein's Department Store (in the center, and on the north side after 1932), Bennett Jewelers (south), and (for a year) the Liggett Drug Store (north and corner), this commercial complex attracted typical "cosmetic" Deco lessees. Friezes of undulating lines, rosettes, spandrels of a thick Deco linenfold paneling, and superb voluted Deco capitals comprised its ornament.

Pringle and Smith's other major Art Deco work of the period is another office tower, the W. W. Orr Doctors Building (1930). The serpent and staff panels identify this as a medical building;[7] it was the city's second highrise built specifically for the medical profession, following G. Lloyd Preacher's 1927 Medical Arts Building sited just farther south along Peachtree Street.

The Orr Building's corner location had been occupied since 1904 by the four-story Marlborough Apartments, one of the city's earliest grand apartment buildings. In 1911, the Davis-Fischer Sanatorium,[8] located on Crew Street since the turn of the century, moved into new facilities just to the north of the Marlborough Apartments. A seven-story addition to the sanatorium was projected for 1923, and in response to the sanatorium's development, the nearby Marlborough Apartment building was converted to doctors' offices. A fire in April 1930, however, destroyed the Marlborough and its contents, including irreplaceable records and valuable medical equipment. A committee of former tenants, led by Dr. F. Phinizy Calhoun, began to plan a modern, fireproof, eleven-story office building for doctors and dentists to include a ground-floor arcade of four shops, a parking garage, and a formal garden.

The Marlborough Company, owner of the apartment-turned-doctors' building, had

W. W. Orr Building,
Pringle and Smith, 1930
(photo from Robert M.
Craig Collection, Atlanta
History Center)

been founded by Atlanta businessmen George P. Howard, George Muse, and William W. Orr. Orr was a prominent member of the Chamber of Commerce, former president of the George Muse Clothing Com-

pany, and had lived at the Marlborough for over a decade. He died in 1927, and it was to honor him that the new doctors' building was named the W. W. Orr Building.

The Southern Ferro Concrete Construction

ABOVE: *Asclepius's serpent and staff (symbol of medicine), W. W. Orr Building, Pringle and Smith, 1930 (photo by Robert M. Craig)*

months after the fire destroying the Marlborough), and the first tenants moved in beginning in April 1931.

In the Louis Sullivan tradition, the Orr Building's ornament is concentrated at ground and mezzanine level, at parapet, and between windows in panels. In the six central bays, windows and corrugated panels are recessed so that five vertical piers (at the same plane as the two side bays) extend from base to skyline in order "to emphasize the tallness of the tall building," as Sullivan would encourage skyscraper designers to do. This subtle treatment of the central bays is further accented with panels of radiating sunbursts at parapet level. The monochromatic ornament, set against cream-colored brick, draws the observer's attention to a simpler array of architectural accents: not the brightly colored, glazed terra-cotta patterns of traditionally picturesque Deco, but the abstraction of machine-cut, incised patterns defined by light and shadow, not color. Springing from a Modernistic aesthetic linked to technology as well as to nature, such Art Deco detail appears machine-faceted more than organic, mechanistic more than hand-crafted, and abstract in its pattern.

This ideal of the machine in service to art parallels the effort to engineer the W. W. Orr

Company, who the previous year had finished the Rhodes-Haverty Building, was selected to build the reinforced-concrete, Deco-ornamented structure, which Pringle and Smith hastily designed. The construction contract was dated July 1930 (just three

AT RIGHT: *Ornament, W. W. Orr Building, Pringle and Smith, 1930 (photo by Robert M. Craig)*

Building in the most up-to-date, fireproof materials. Both Wachendorff at the Davis-Fischer Sanatorium and Pringle and Smith at the Orr Building selected brick as a protection from fire. The devastating 1917 Atlanta fire, which had destroyed some three hundred acres and 1,938 buildings, was a fresh memory that discouraged wood-frame construction throughout the 1920s. Moreover, it becomes increasingly evident that Atlanta physicians and dentists during the Deco-to-Modern period repeatedly built offices, clinics, and hospitals that combined the most current architectural stylistic imagery with progressive construction, turning by the 1940s to an avant-garde Modern aesthetic for smaller-scaled professional buildings. But for now, the shift to a modern image was conservative: the restrained classical trim of Preacher's Medical Arts Building became the restrained Art Deco modern of the W. W. Orr Building.

The lower two floors of the building are marked by limestone facing above a polished granite base, capped by a terra-cotta frieze. The Peachtree Street entry is framed in black granite with fluted granite quarter-columns *in antis* and flanked by elaborate light fixtures whose relief decoration appears to transform classical volutes and acroteria into organic plant forms (see p. 24 and colorplate). A simple form from a distance, the W. W. Orr Building rewards close inspection, disclosing an array of Art Deco enrichment inside and out.

The period of 1929-30 was one of extraordinary skyscraper construction in Atlanta, with firms other than Pringle and Smith also

participating in the city's tall-building development. Although never achieving its projected height nor full impact, the Southern Bell Building (AT&T Communications Building) of 1929 was intended, at twenty-five stories, to be Atlanta's premier Modernistic skyscraper. With setbacks beginning at the seventh floor and reoccurring at various stages above, and with its smooth limestone surfaces, much of the formal impact was to rely on light and shadow contrasts and on profile rather than on color. Southern Bell looks back to the ziggurat tower setbacks of post-1916 New York skyscrapers[9] and forward to the neo-Deco profiles and light effects of the 1992 GLG Building in Atlanta. Hugh Ferriss, during the Deco period, sketched dramatic urban towers with shadowy setbacks and weighty forms, and Southern Bell, if built to its full height, would have achieved for Atlanta a noble pile of monumental Modernistic forms.

However, Southern Bell's downtown office tower opened in 1930 at only six stories (exclusive of basement and sub-basement); it was raised in 1947 and 1948 to fourteen, and was marred by a tower addition in 1963, which one tries fruitlessly to erase mentally each time the building is now

viewed. The building was designed by Marye, Alger, and Vinour, fresh from their triumph at the Fox Theatre in Atlanta (1929). If the exotic spirit of the Deco era takes explicit form in Vinour's designs at the Fox, then Art Deco's machine-cut faceted aesthetic achieves in the ornament of the Southern Bell Building its finest moment in Atlanta (see colorplates). Here, geometric ornaments and stylized sculptural respresentations of birds and human forms are unsurpassed among Deco buildings in the South, including Miami Beach.[10] The keystone above the Mayan-inspired corbeled entry is a masterpiece of Deco abstraction, and the lobby's

ABOVE: *Drawing by Hugh Ferriss from* The Metropolis of Tomorrow *(1929) (courtesy of Ives Washburn, Publisher)*

FACING PAGE: *Architect's rendering, original design, Southern Bell Building, Marye, Alger, and Vinour, 1929 (courtesy of the Atlanta History Center)*

AT LEFT: *Ornament, Southern Bell Building, Marye, Alger, and Vinour, 1929 (photo from Robert M. Craig Collection, Atlanta History Center)*

elaborate linear patterns enrich the elevator doors and radiator grills.

The sixth floor of the Southern Bell Building contained "the largest long distance telephone switchboard in the South." While no local calls were to be handled at the facility, the building housed "the complicated equipment required for long distance telephone service, telegraph equipment, the devices used in sending and receiving pictures by wire, and the control apparatus for the various radio broadcasting systems operating in Atlanta." The radio room was on the third floor. It included a control board employed by the Columbia Broadcasting System (CBS), associated locally with WGST, and a second board used for the National Broadcasting Company (NBC), affiliated with WSB in Atlanta and WAM in Birmingham. The third floor also housed an impressive array of telephone repeaters, "with their hundreds of glowing vacuum tube filaments"—equipment that amplified sound, making long distance telephony possible.[11]

Other technical features, reflecting the latest developments, ensured that the building was modern in functional as well as aesthetic terms. Nearby Georgia Power plants supplied electricity, which was controlled for the building by two large boards in the basement and which operated two groups of motor generator sets to charge Southern Bell's enormous batteries. Including the liquid electrolyte, these batteries weighed 130 tons, and 40-ton copper bars connected the batteries to the control boards. Although the steel-frame and limestone building was fireproof, an emergency fire pump, able to jet water the height of a fifty-story building, would protect the Southern Bell Building inside and out. An emergency gaslighting system was provided. Two automatic elevators of the latest high-speed type were placed in immediate service when the building opened, although seventeen were projected to be required when the twenty-five story structure was completed.[12]

Operator comfort was especially of concern to designers. Controlled fresh air, heated and filtered to remove dust, was changed in the building every eight to ten minutes. Soundproofing material on the walls and ceiling helped to silence the busy confusion of scores of operators talking simultaneously. The sub-basement contained an automotive refrigerator to cool drinking water supplied to the building. A registered nurse was on duty as health supervisor and personal advisor to the female operators, and a matron and maids were in attendance on the fifth floor, where a sitting room, "quiet room," lavatories, shower baths, and locker rooms "furnished in the modern style" were available to serve the staff. The fifth-floor suite of staff service rooms also included a cafeteria, a 1,700-square-foot "tastefully decorated" dining room, and a kitchen "that would delight the heart of any woman."[13]

The Southern Bell Building stood as a symbol of progress in a modern city. During the Deco era, electricity, telephony, radio transmission, air travel, etc., offered icons to an age of scientific advancement. This building was to be a Deco landmark culminating

a half-century development of telephone operation in the city, a development that resulted in an extensive system of long-distance lines terminating in Atlanta.

The city's first telephone was installed in 1877 to connect the Western and Atlantic freight depot with Durand's restaurant in the Union Passenger Station downtown. Within seven years there were 400 subscribers in Atlanta, and the first long-distance line connected Atlanta to nearby Decatur, Georgia. By 1930, the year after the new building opened, the Chamber of Commerce noted that 89 percent of the world's telephones (31.5 million of the 35.2 million) "can now be connected to any telephone in Atlanta."

Atlanta's long-distance facility now connected the city to "twenty-three European countries, Canada, part of Mexico and Australia and three countries in South America." Fifteen direct circuits to Macon and Birmingham, seven to New York City, five to Chicago, Miami, and Cincinnati, and others to St. Louis, Detroit, Dallas, and elsewhere ensured a rapid increase in telephone traffic from and to Atlanta. Perhaps, above all, what this building represented to Atlanta telephone users was an adjustment in the practice of making a call: no longer was an order placed with an operator who made the connection at a specified time and phoned back to connect the originating caller; now one waited on the line for an almost immediate connection. The average time to complete a call had been reduced from 9.8 minutes in 1925 to 2.4 minutes in 1930.[14]

The Modernistic setback image of the telephone building was to be echoed in visionary construction projects elsewhere in downtown Atlanta. A new Louis Dinkler Hotel, by G. Lloyd Preacher of Atlanta and Thompson, Holmes, and Converse of New York, was projected by Carling Dinkler, head of the Dinkler Hotel Company, for the southeast corner of Peachtree and Ellis streets. This was the former site of the six-story, 125-room Aragon Hotel, built by George W. Collier in 1892 and demolished in 1930.

Entrepreneurs had sought to no avail to buy the Aragon Hotel land, one inquiring of Collier if the applicant's covering the lot with silver dollars would buy the property. Collier reportedly said that it would, *if* the silver dollars were stood on edge![15] One wonders whether it was such reluctance to close a deal, or the depression, that doomed the Dinkler. The architect's drawing of the projected Dinkler Hotel, however, showed a proud monument of spirited Deco design, a Modernistic setback block rising twenty floors to a central tower. The 750-room hotel was never constructed, however; instead, the Collier Building was erected on the site, since replaced by the Georgia Pacific Center and the Peachtree Center MARTA Station.

Envisioning that it would someday front a great plaza covering the railroad tracks, architects projected in 1930 the United States Warehouse Company Building, a dramatic

setback tower, for the former site of Atlanta's Union Station. The building would face west and was hoped to overlook Bleckley Plaza, a civic piazza proposed in 1909 (and repeatedly since) by architect Harrison Bleckley. Bleckley Plaza was to be a monumental piazza transforming adjacent rail tracks into a more urbane open space. The U.S. Warehouse Company Building, containing a large cold-storage plant and offices, would use air rights over the railroad and state property and was projected to cost $3.5 million. However, neither the Modernistic warehouse nor Bleckley Plaza were to be built.

G. Lloyd Preacher, whose Dinkler Hotel was never erected, *was* able to construct a masterpiece of Deco skyscraper architecture in 1930 when he completed his Atlanta City Hall. This aspiring Deco-Gothic tower provided the city with a representation in steel frame and terra-cotta of Atlanta's symbol, the "phoenix rising from ashes," referring not only to the city's recovery from General Sherman's Civil War burning,[16] but also to the city's reconstruction since its devastating 1917 fire. The Atlanta City Seal (containing a phoenix and the inscription *1845 Resurgens 1867*) is set within the ornamental terra-cotta panels at two levels of the building's elevation. As a symbol of Atlanta's "rise from the flames," Preacher's City Hall was also a landmark of the city's new Deco-era civic pride.

In 1925 the Chamber of Commerce began its Forward Atlanta campaign, promoting civic improvement and commercial expansion. The economic growth of the city was reflected in subsequent transformations of the downtown skyline, marking the commercial energy of an expanding Atlanta: by 1930, *The City Builder* noted, construction was so extensive that "in almost every business block the pedestrian finds himself forced off the sidewalk by building operations—a new structure or improvements to an old building."[17] The Forward Atlanta campaign especially brought focus to (beyond economic growth) the city's civic pride and image. Attention was drawn in

particular to the need for a new City Hall, which could become a monument to the city's advancement and position as the leader of a New South.

In the fall of 1925, *The City Builder* published views of recent building projects

TOP RIGHT: *City Hall, G. Lloyd Preacher, 1929-30 (photo by Robert M. Craig)*

BOTTOM RIGHT: *Nebraska State Capitol, Lincoln, Bertram Goodhue, 1929-32 (photo by G. Condra, courtesy of the Nebraska State Historical Society)*

across the nation that would influence Atlanta architects, much as they proved influential throughout the country. Bertram Goodhue's Nebraska State Capitol project, housing government in a skyscraper tower, appeared in the October 1925 issue. The Nebraska Capitol became an important Deco-era landmark and would have significant influence on "Depression Modern" forms of a stripped-down "Modern Classic" aesthetic during the thirties.

Moreover, in its towered form, Goodhue's state capitol presented a progressive model for government architecture, an image that replaced the more typically neoclassical and domed capitol model with a vertical tower. Capitols (including the one Georgia had built in Atlanta in 1889), city halls, county courthouses, and similar government structures had traditionally been designed as historicist, classical revival buildings, but the modern skyscraper would now offer a new prototype for a twentieth-century government architecture.[18]

The appropriation of the skyscraper for governmental architecture reflected significant changes already occurring in the role of government in Americans' lives. At all levels of government, a new type of official architecture presented itself to be as much an administrative office building as civic monument. The commercial skyscraper or office tower lacked an image of inherent monumentality, unlike a neoclassical edifice, domed and porticoed; the skyscraper was less likely to communicate an image nobly expressive of statesmanship and civic pride traditionally associated with government architecture in the classical mode. What the skyscraper form for state capitols or city halls did communicate was that lawmakers and administrators, and the official houses they inhabited, were becoming increasingly bureaucratic.

The skyscraper suggested that the modern halls of government were to be filled with less oratory and more paperwork, less statesmanly leadership and more bureaucratic conformity, less ritual and more procedure, and *much* more processing of reports, claims, files, records, and forms. Architecturally, the message was that instead of a progression of columned halls, noble domed rotundas, and ceremonial *grandes salles des pas perdus*, the office of state was to be a bureaucratic skyscraper.

However, the ennobling of its stacked office floors of clerical cells, the dressing of these governmental towers with historic architectural garb, might well enhance the skyscraper's role as a civic monument. In considering the *proper* dress for the occasion, Atlanta's leading architect, A. Ten Eyck Brown, projected as early as June 1925 "a Modern Idea for the New City Hall whenever Atlana Can Have One."[19] The modernity of his project was that it was a twenty-story skyscraper; it was also a grand exercise in Beaux-Arts Classicism intended for the block east of Brown's earlier 1911-14 Fulton County Courthouse. Brown's unexecuted city hall project stacked up three graduated blocks: from a wide three-story-plus-mezzanine base, with monumental columned loggia entries, rose thirteen additional floors of offices to a setback, pyramid-topped crown of four floors, this latter capping the whole with a form reminiscent of the ancient mausoleum at Halicarnassus. When it came time to commission the city hall, however, Brown's traditionalist image was displaced by a more progressive Deco tower, and G. Lloyd Preacher would be the architect of Atlanta's built City Hall.

In contrast with both Brown's classical city hall tower proposal (published in June of 1925) and Goodhue's stripped classicism in Nebraska (published in Atlanta in October 1925), Atlanta's executed City Hall was to be dressed in Gothic, albeit Deco-Gothic. The same issue of *The City Builder* that published Goodhue's Nebraska Capitol also published two influential neo-Gothic towers—the winning entry in the *Chicago Tribune* competition by the architectural firm Hood and Howells, and Charles Klauder's Cathedral of Learning proposal for the University of Pittsburgh. Both adapted explicitly Gothic forms and ornament to the skyscraper, and may be considered sources for Atlanta's City Hall.

Other neo-Gothic towers offered models for Atlanta. Architects Morgan and Dillon had employed medieval shafts and Gothic decorative details on the Healey Building completed in 1913 in Atlanta. About the same time in New York, Cass Gilbert had clad his fifty-five-story Woolworth Building (1911-13) in terra-cotta dress. The landmark steel-frame tower, with its historic detail and neo-Gothic decoration at various setbacks, echoed the chateauesque Gothic of Louis XII Blois. And contemporary with Preacher's own neo-Gothic Atlanta City Hall tower was the Sterick Building of 1928-30 in Memphis, Tennessee, at twenty-nine floors and 365 feet the tallest skyscraper in the South when completed.

Much as Goodhue in Nebraska brought a neoclassical vocabulary to a stripped-down modern skyscraper form, so Preacher in Atlanta would combine historic medieval ele-

ments with the progressive forms of the Deco skyscraper. Elements also recall Eliel Saarinen's second-prize *Chicago Tribune* competition entry, a project whose spirit and architectural forms reverberated nationally when published in the mid-1920s. Like Saarinen's project, Atlanta City Hall synthesizes a Gothic verticality, a Sullivanesque organization of ornament, and setback forms inspired by the 1916 New York zoning legislation, a prime influence on 1920s ziggurat profiles on skyscrapers nationally. Preacher's City Hall differs substantially from Saarinen's project in its historical formal language—Preacher's building was a terra-cotta-encrusted, neo-Gothic cathedral of municipal administration—but like Saarinen's masterful proposal for Chicago, Atlanta City Hall was intended to embody in its vertical forms the energetic aspirations of a competitive city.

ABOVE: *City Hall, G. Lloyd Preacher, 1929-30 (photo by Robert M. Craig)*

ABOVE RIGHT: *Second-prize entry,* Chicago Tribune *competition, Eliel Saarinen, 1922 (courtesy of Rizzoli International)*

Passage of a $1 million bond issue in 1926, during I. E. Ragsdale's mayoral administration, made construction of the City Hall possible, and G. Lloyd Preacher was commissioned to design the structure. South Carolinian by birth and education (he graduated from Clemson University in 1904), G. Lloyd Preacher began practicing architecture in 1910 in Augusta, Georgia, building that city's first skyscraper, the Marion Building, in 1912. He moved to Atlanta in 1922 and would eventually open offices in Indianapolis, Memphis, Raleigh, Spartanburg, St. Petersburg, Miami, New York, and San Francisco. His hotels, apartment buildings, schools, and office buildings are located throughout the Southeast; he was to become one of the region's most significant institutional and commercial architects.[20]

Preacher's City Hall is a composition of primary, secondary, and tertiary vertical piers in a rhythm of shafts that establish principal bays, corner setbacks, and a lively energy in the elevations. A cathedral-porch-like entry ennobles the Mitchell Street entrance, projecting forward to receive visitors like the Gothic porch at Ely Cathedral but here styled in a more decorative terra-cotta molding with cuspate canopy arches and flanking lamp stanchions of Deco inspiration. Balcony-like forms are affixed at principal compositional levels of the building to organize the facade in larger units, and the building's ornamental use of cuspate arches and other fourteenth-century detail combines the cosmetic nature of Deco with historicism. The

Entry porch, City Hall, G. Lloyd Preacher, 1929-30 (photo by Robert M. Craig)

narthex porch floor is pink marble, the walls terra-cotta, and the ceiling framed by colorful moldings. Door transoms are rich with Gothic tracery, and original chandeliers survive as Gothic lanterns.

The lobby (see colorplates), like Deco-era lobbies of office buildings and movie houses, is theatrical, enriched by transforming decorative elements that stimulate romantic imaginations in an effort to purge the building of its commercial or institutional character. The City Hall lobby extends between two grand marble staircases and focuses on elaborate bronze elevator doors and their rich enframements. Walls and pillars are of polished coquina marble from Brunswick, Georgia—the staircase marble is from Tate, Georgia—and the room is crowned with an elaborate painted ceiling of carved and gilded wood. Ornamental beamed ceilings, with stenciling, also enriched the mayor's suite and city council chambers on the second floor, but the only other interior space to rival the narthex and lobby is the fee-collecting department opening beneath a marble arch and through traceried doors to the east of the lobby, rich in bronze fittings.

City Hall opened February 22, 1930, just two months after the opening of the Atlanta Fox Theatre, and both stand today as embodiments of Atlanta's Deco-era exuberance, its romance, its cosmetic colorism, and its fantasy. Both became landmarks of civic

AT LEFT: *Window ornament and parapet detail, City Hall, G. Lloyd Preacher, 1929-30 (photo by Robert M. Craig)*

pride. However, neither reflected any awareness of the Great Crash, whose "Black Tuesday" in October occurred just as both buildings were nearing completion. In that sense, both may be seen today as swan songs of the Roaring Twenties, theatrical Deco-era fantasies of an escapism not yet awakened by the reality of the depressed thirties.

Art Deco architecture has especially been considered a "skyscraper style."[21] Most certainly, in considering Atlanta towers of 1929-30 (Southern Bell, the William-Oliver Building, the W. W. Orr Building, and City Hall, as well as the unexecuted Dinkler Hotel and the U.S. Warehouse Company Building), Atlanta's Art Deco architecture focuses on the skyscraper. But two buildings of ordinary function, at the smaller scale of two to three floors, survive today on side streets of Atlanta where (abandoned or reduced to downtown parking-garage function) they remain unnoticed.

The Troy Peerless Laundry Building was constructed in 1928-29 to serve increased numbers of hotels and apartment buildings erected along Ponce de Leon Avenue during the 1920s. At the time, that corridor was

developing as a connection between midtown Atlanta and the Druid Hills neighborhood.[22] This was a period of extensive apartment development in the city, and Ponce de Leon Avenue was a prime east-side location for such development.[23] The Troy Peerless commercial laundry responded to the increased demand for commercial laundering of bed and table linen during a period when this service was seldom provided "in house." As a commercial advertisement, it packaged its mundane service function in a building of the latest Art Deco image and made a laundry stylish.

Troy Peerless was a reinforced concrete and brick industrial building whose architect, Isaac Moscowitz, designed a facade adorned in Art Deco trim within a classical organization. The craftsmanship in brickmasonry is remarkable. Panels of basket-weave brick accented with small polychromatic terra-cotta insets brought color and pattern to a structure that could easily have remained ordinary and dull. Bricks set at angles to create a continuous vertical fluting of facade piers reinforced the classical imagery, which established an order and a certain stateliness

Troy Peerless Laundry Building, Isaac Moscowitz, 1928-29 (photo from Robert M. Craig Collection, Atlanta History Center)

in the building. The fluted piers were topped with polychromatic terra-cotta capitals with abstract volutes in a Deco-transformed Ionic (see colorplate). The white classicism of the door enframements and base, the pilastered facade, and the polychrome-enriched decorative cornice brought an assured presence to this masterwork of Atlanta Deco; the building demands to be preserved as one of the city's best smaller-scaled works of this phase of popular Deco modernism.

Even more inconspicuous on its back street and overwhelmed by adjacent towers of Peachtree Center is the C. E. Freeman Ford Auto Agency Building (1930), designed by G. Lloyd Preacher and now a parking garage on Houston Street. Its ordinary industrial character reflects the first phase of automobile showroom architecture, simple masonry structures not unlike the automobile assembly plants themselves.[24] In such simple structures as the Freeman Ford Agency, "machines" of the first automobile age were displayed, sold, and repaired.

The Freeman Ford Agency is saved from being a mundane, easily ignored, industrial building by the delicate Art Deco frieze of polychromatic terra-cotta that enriches its upper facade (see colorplate). A lineup of blossoming flowers on upright stems regularly interspersed with abstract Deco patterns creates a remarkable stencil-like border. Variegated colors on brick surfaces produce a tapestry effect, where uniform bricks might have created a dull factory aesthetic. The Houston Street Ford agency may be condemned today to the ordinary function of a parking garage, but it remains as well a relic of Deco craftsmanship all too infrequently preserved in Atlanta.

At this smaller scale, Art Deco found particular reception in "main street" commercial architecture. Regenstein's Department Store of 1929, discussed above, represents a major building type for Art Deco architecture evidenced at a more pedestrian scale in cities throughout the country. Department stores and various retail emporia, five-and-dimes, drugstores, and sundries outlets along

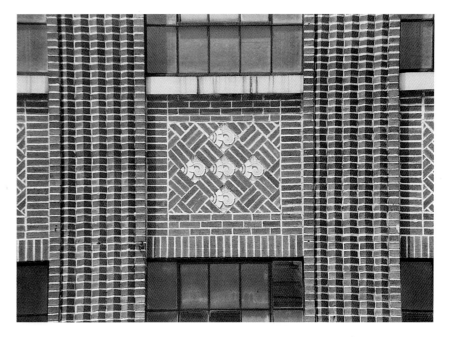

American commercial streets found that their businesses benefited from the colorful Deco stylisms. Deco attracted attention and thus had substantial advertisement appeal. New facades on older commercial buildings began to display "modernized" resurfacing in terra-cotta and, later, Vitrolite. In an effort to effect a contemporary image, Main Street architecture in the 1930s was being "made up" in various Art Deco images by applying a Deco cosmetic to building facades.

Two Kress buildings in Atlanta reflect varying images of such new facades. The Atlanta Urban Design Commission rightfully

TOP: *Brick and terra-cotta ornament, Troy Peerless Laundry Building, Isaac Moscowitz, 1928-29 (photo by Robert M. Craig)*

MIDDLE: *C. E. Freeman Ford Agency, G. Lloyd Preacher, 1930 (photo from Robert M. Craig Collection, Atlanta History Center)*

has called the Kress Building (1933) at 1012-14 Peachtree Street "a textbook example of the Art Deco style in a commercial building."[25] Architect Edward F. Sibbert, who "Deco-ized" Kress stores throughout the region,[26] surfaced the complete street facade of a narrow and deep masonry building with glazed terra-cotta. The face-lift was accented further by colorful insets of polychromatic terra-cotta and beveled corners. The Kress insignia identified the store at the center top framed by chevron inset panels set on edge to serve as brackets for the lettering. Atop the narrow window at each end was placed another inset panel of abstract design. The uniformity of the cream tile and symmetrically balanced fenestration provided a classical order to the storefront, and it was this smooth regularity that was repeated in the new Kress store, three years later, at 67-71 Peachtree downtown.

The 1936 Kress reflects the more restrained, monochromatic face of the depression years and is part of a street of several noteworthy modern commercial buildings of the period. At Mangel's (1935) several devices invite potential customers into the store: the movement and flow of abstract wavy lines in the terrazzo floor, the spacious two-story volume open to the street, the large graphics, and the shop windows of large plate glass displaying goods in uncluttered modern settings. The whole looks forward to even more reduced forms

and clean lines of late-forties Modernism.

Nearby, McCrory's Department Store of ca. 1936-37 covers a late Victorian building with a new facade whose classically inspired central bay projects forward, while the parapet steps down in Deco "zigzag"

McCrory's Department Store, 1936-37 (photo from Robert M. Craig Collection, Atlanta History Center)

fashion. Ribbed surfaces on recessed panels in the center bays achieve a layered look. Bold and simple, both McCrory's and the 1936 Kress Building next door acknowledged the restrained spirit of thirties Deco.

In the Kress Building, Deco incisions and a classical orderliness and simplicity were balanced with vertical ribbed piers presenting recognizable features found in Kress Buildings in Durham, North Carolina, Richmond,

doors, which were in turn capped by a glazed panel of wavy vertical lines and sculptural accent. Above the entry Julian H. Harris carved a central panel of rampant squirrels flanking a disc, and an owl perched within a panel niche on either side.

While the Morris Plan Bank does not survive (the 1959-61 Bank of Georgia Building is today on the site), there are extant commercial structures, contemporary with Mc-Crory's, the downtown Kress store, and the Morris Plan Bank, whose restrained facades define a Deco aesthetic distinctly different from the exuberant 1929-30 designs of Pringle and Smith. Architect Cyril B. Smith constructed a store at 82-84 Broad Street in late 1937 whose Deco detail is limited to a simple frieze atop a very plain facade. The Decatur Chevrolet Company (Leiphart Chevrolet, now the National Business Institute Building) was built in 1936 and employed Deco-period setback profiles for its central entry bay as well as for the ornamental crowns of the four principal structural piers. The simplified forms and depression-era restraint of such works give evidence of a later phase of Deco.

Contemporary with these structures is Atlanta's only residence in the Deco image, a mid-depression synthesis of Art Deco foliate panels, linear pattern, and setback profiles, and the restrained "Depression Modern" of the mid-thirties. This aesthetic, as department stores nationally provide evidence, promoted essentially a commercial rather than residential style. Certainly Art Deco informed residential interiors; its stylish veneers and appliqués entered the boudoir and bath, and, as a progressive *art décoratif*, the Art Deco aesthetic was popular in domestic decorative arts and furnishings. Mirrors, exotic woods, zigzag fixtures, and foliate ornament decorated the most private spaces of homes, which found models to emulate in the chic movie sets of Astaire and Rogers films. The application of exterior commercial Deco to house design during the thirties was exceptional,[27] however, and in this respect the Evans-Cucich House of 1934 is unique in Atlanta.

Located in a traditional neighborhood on

ABOVE: *Morris Plan Bank, Tucker and Howell, 1936 (relief sculpture by Julian H. Harris) (photo courtesy of Women's Chamber of Commerce of Atlanta)*

Virginia, and elsewhere throughout the Southeast.

This mid-thirties spirit of a simplified Deco is evidenced in a small bank designed by Tucker and Howell and built in 1936 on Peachtree Street next door to the more exuberant Art Deco William-Oliver Building of six years earlier. The Morris Plan Bank was a one-story structure of plain surface ornamented with delicate lines, which both enframed the recessed entry and delineated an attic level, providing the facade's distinctly classical proportions. Atop the parapet rested the large letters spelling *Morris Plan Bank*. Curved glass windows provided a transition to the paired metal and glass

Decatur (later Southern) Chevrolet Company (Leiphart Chevrolet), 1936 (photo by Robert M. Craig)

BELOW: *Evans-Cucich House, A. F. N. Everett, 1934 (photo from Robert M. Craig Collection, Atlanta History Center)*

Relief ornament, Evans-Cucich House, A. F. N. Everett, 1934 (photo by Robert M. Craig, courtesy of Atlanta Urban Design Commission)

example, the Five Points intersection of Birmingham, Alabama, or a commercial strip of South Miami Beach. The aesthetic squirms uncomfortably as it sits on a shaded suburban street lined with historic revival homes.

The Evans-Cucich House was built as the idiosyncratic residence for Hiram Evans, the Imperial Wizard of the Ku Klux Klan.[28] The house was designed by A. F. N. Everett, whose early 1920s apartments and churches were monumentally Beaux-Arts Classical, who built houses in the 1920s in the romantic Mediterranean Style, and who now turned to a progressive and colorful image, ornamenting the surfaces of Evans' house with what the architect's son has called "modern Egyptian motifs."[29] The main entry facing Peachtree Battle Avenue was flanked by fluted piers, the window above was framed by flat setback moldings, and a minimal cornice topped the restrained facade at the flat roof. The house was surfaced in limestone and displays a noteworthy bas-relief with stylized floral arrangements on its west elevation; zigzag profiles abound inside and out.

The interior (see colorplates) was organized around a central stairhall with the elegant curved staircase now lighted by a Deco-era chandelier from a New York hotel. Applied zigzag panels, whose profiles suggest a miniaturized, inverted Empire State Building, ornament the hall. A major cross axis of open space joins the stairhall with living room and dining room, the three spaces identified by the three large ground-floor windows of the main facade. In recent years a Minoan-inspired mural has enriched the breakfast room with an archaic imagery not incompatible with Art Deco, whose stylists would find in such early Aegean cultures a flat decorative primitivism comparable to the colorful pre-Columbian surface effects that Deco-era artists, engaged in the Mayan Revival, frequently borrowed.

As we have noted, Art Deco especially found reception in public buildings frequented by the masses—the lobbies of office buildings, the local department stores, and

a parkway designed by Beaux-Arts architects Carrère and Hastings, the Evans-Cucich House presented a commercial image of dense blocky forms and colorless surfaces conspicuously displaying a modern (even nonresidential) taste on an otherwise traditional suburban streetscape. The house combined setback corners and profiles, a facade of classic symmetry with thin accenting pilaster buttresses, and a Mayanesque cubic compactness. Like Mayan architecture, these surfaces were incised with abstract foliate ornament, barely noticed linear relief patterns on an extraordinary residence of the thirties. All these features appear more at home in the commercial streetscape of, for

Interior, Evans-Cucich House, A. F. N. Everett, 1934 (photo by Robert M. Craig)

the downtown and smaller neighborhood movie theaters. Several Deco theaters were designed in the 1930s in Atlanta reflecting the national popularity of the style among theatergoers (and certainly best evidenced at Radio City Music Hall of 1931-32 in New York). The Loew's Grand Theatre, occupying the historic 1893 DeGive Grand Opera House on Peachtree Street, remodeled its interior in 1932 to bring it up to date with the progressive and popular style for modern movie theaters.

The designer was Thomas Lamb, who in 1929 had been the architect of the San Francisco Fox in a neo-Baroque style; who designed in New York the Loew's State, the Academy of Music, the Rialto, the Rivoli, and the Capitol theaters; and who, by the early thirties, "had successfully meandered through every conceivable expression of theater architecture—including the Byzantine, the French Baroque, a thorough study of the style of the Adam brothers, and unabashed Oriental-Hindu, as seen in the Loew's 72nd Street theater, New York."[30] Lamb was now turning to new Deco images,[31] and Atlanta's exercise of the mid-thirties was to be "moderne on a budget."[32]

Lamb transformed a grand opera house to a Deco movie theater, and in so doing the theater came to symbolize the passing of the baton from a history-based fine art to modernism. The artistry of muralist Paolo Payesich, who is said to have decorated the Sultan's Palace in Constantinople and the Czar's Palace in St. Petersburg, had created for the 1893 opera house a proscenium decoration of eight allegorical figures narrating "the triumph of Fantasy, Poetry, and Music." Lamb did employ allegorical figures in the lobby, where wood veneer murals depicted two-dimensional, almost

Egyptian figures representing government, justice, music, agriculture, and industry, the latter symbolized by a mechanical cog-wheel. But for the auditorium, Lamb looked to New York's Radio City Music Hall in treating the ceiling in graduated tiers of chevrons in a room of warm plums, beiges, browns, and bright orange, "colors first juxtaposed in modern art by the Fauvist painters like Matisse." The stage curtain, originally depicting a scene of Shakespeare reading a play before Queen Elizabeth, now

displayed across its asbestos surfaces multicolored zigzags echoing the elongated chevrons that framed the proscenium. The loges and box of the opera house gave way to Lamb's preferred single deep balcony. And throughout, the stencils, light fixtures, pendants, and Deco ornament reflected a new theater with a new policy. The legitimate theater of 1893-1916, followed by the vaudeville with silent pictures of 1916-28, was now to be a sound-motion-picture-only venue, "without stage shows or *extraneous*

music to detract from the pictures." The historic DeGive Opera House had been modernized to become an Art Deco movie house.[33]

The Loew's Grand was located next door to the Paramount Theater built by Hentz, Reid, and Adler in 1920 as the Howard Theater. By the end of 1926, Peachtree Street was being called the "Broadway of the South,"[34] and soon two multistoried neon marquees were lighting up the night streetscape of Atlanta's Broadway with the towering supergraphics of *Paramount* and *Loew's Grand*. The neon lights of Peachtree brightened the depression years of the thirties with offerings of celluloid escapism. As a display, the neon of these marquees was matched only, perhaps, by the city's famed circular neon sign for Coca Cola, flashing red and white light northward from the Candler Building and recently recalled in the neo-Deco rotating neon sign at the World of Coca Cola Pavilion (Underground Atlanta).

So many great movie houses have been lost nationally. Atlanta, like other cities impacted by television, multitheaters, and video movie rentals, has witnessed its movie palaces suffering from the same architectural vandalizing (the suburban mauling of movie environments) that plagues downtown and neighborhood cinemas around the country. The Paramount in Atlanta was razed in 1960, and a twelve-story building (immediately characterized as having no architectural distinction) replaced it.[35] In January 1978, the Loew's Grand suffered a major fire, which fire inspectors suspected had started in more than one location inside, and rising preservation hopes to save the historic structure were squashed. A demolition permit was issued immediately in February, and the grand old opera house-turned-Deco movie palace was demolished, its bricks, at least, collected for dubious preservation purposes. Because the theater had served as the showcase for the premiere showing of the film *Gone with the Wind*, the building's bricks were sold to souvenir hunters seeking to own a piece of history. Few seemed to realize, as prefire efforts to save the building proved fruitless, that all

Atlanta owned a piece of this grand old building for reasons that transcended the price of a brick.

Across the country, however, some masterpieces of Deco theater design survive, none surpassing the Paramount Theater in Oakland, California, and Radio City Music Hall in New York City. But it was at the more intimate scale of the smaller neighborhood movie theater that Deco found its widest popular reception in the era following the grandiose "atmospheric" movie palaces.

Atlanta built several such small theaters at the end of the depression and on the eve of World War II.[36] Plaza Theater, a part of a 1939 suburban shopping center which will be discussed in the following volume, opened its neon fan of Deco zigzag edges to provide a focus at the center of the storefronts at Briarcliff Plaza. The colorful unfolding of the serrated fan, by orchestrated sequential lighting of ribs of neon, drew attention to the theater in a theatrical way. "The Plaza" remains Atlanta's best surviving neighborhood Art Deco theater. The following year the Little Five Points Theater was built at the edge of the small commercial business district northeast of Inman Park, and immediately afterward (1940-41) the adjacent Euclid Theater was erected. The facades were accented by simple marquees, marked in the Little Five Points Theater by a vertical fin, in the Euclid Theater by an arrangement of tubular ornaments composed like splayed organ pipes to establish a Deco setback profile. Such vertical accents, especially the fin marquee, served as an erect landmark during the early age of the automobile to arrest the fast horizontal flow of the speeding car along the roadway. The marquee became a visual mast for theaters, bus depots, roadside diners, and the like. In Atlanta, in 1940, marquees were built on the Little Five Points Theater, the downtown Greyhound Bus Depot, and the Varsity Restaurant, the last two among Atlanta's finest period works of roadside Streamlined Moderne.

Art Deco was essentially a cosmetic, and often architects resurfaced building facades in order to refashion the image of an established business. Daniell and Beutell, who

TOP LEFT: *Euclid Theater, 1940-41 (photo by Robert M. Craig)*

TOP RIGHT: *Forsyth-Walton Building, resurfaced by Daniell and Beutell, 1936 (photo by Robert M. Craig)*

BELOW: *Retail Credit Company Building, Morgan and Dillon, 1919-20; Morgan, Dillon, and Lewis, 1929-30 (photo by Robert M. Craig)*

began practice in Atlanta in 1919, plastered over the Forsyth-Walton Building in 1936, giving it the smooth simplicity of the mid-thirties aesthetic. The brick building had stood on its southwest corner site (Forsyth and Walton streets) for over a dozen years, but Daniell and Beutell transformed its utilitarian masonry surfaces to the new fashionable Deco by molding decorative friezes, stepped frames for recessed panels atop windows, and a flat leafage of the Deco-volute or wave-motif variety. The new cosmetic brought the building up to date.

Two works by the well-established firm of

Morgan, Dillon, and Lewis provide similar evidence of both client and architect being brought up to date to the fashionable Deco in changes made to existing buildings. The firm that Edward S. Lewis joined in 1919 dated to the 1882 partnership of Bruce and Morgan (Morgan and Dillon after Bruce retired in 1904), whose numerous early skyscrapers and office buildings survive in the historic Fairlie-Poplar District.[37] In the fall of 1919, Morgan and Dillon began the construction of a reinforced concrete office building for the Retail Credit Company, obtaining a permit to build five stories of a designed nine-story structure. The Southern Ferro Concrete Company, who would later build Pringle and Smith's Rhodes-Haverty and W. W. Orr buildings, finished only three stories by September 1920. It was not until June 1929, however, that the builder added six floors to complete the nine-story tower for (now) Morgan, Dillon, and Lewis. By 1929, the new fashion of Deco was in full bloom, and both the skyline profile and abstracted foliate panels and friezes of the Retail Credit Company Building reflect an *art décoratif* in the spirit of the new, cosmetic ornament. Abstracted linenfold panels on a

field of grape vines appear to step from an Arts-and-Crafts decorative tradition to an Art Deco love of surface pattern; the more organic natural forms become a background in 1929 for an emerging modern abstraction.

In the late summer and early autumn of 1935, Dillon and Lewis repaired a fire-damaged building on Luckie Street, constructed as a pharmacy but known in more recent years to Atlantans as the downtown location of Herrin's Restaurant. Completely au courant, the firm provided a "period" ornament, a fine Art Deco panel employing the era's favorite motifs. From a volute at the base of the panel, a plant with symmetrical leafage and sprouting stem grows toward the stepped-back top of the panel, becoming a fountain of delicate water jets as it pyramids upward.

The make-overs that Art Deco provided for five-and-dimes, for Main Street commercial stores, for theaters and offices and chic boutiques, brought color to the pallid faces of ordinary buildings. Thickly applied in polychromatic terra-cotta, the cosmetic could be gaudy and theatrical; as a light blush it could add romance to an unremarkable streetscape. A kind of architectural makeup, Deco became restrained during the depression years, when the Modernistic became economical and sparse. Faceted with machine-cut precision and formed in syncopated bands of zigzag friezes and setback profiles, the rhythm of Deco could be jazzy and bright. Restrained by the economies of the 1930s, Deco could limit itself to a minimalism that was distinctly modern in its sparseness and abstraction. Its evolution has been described as "the dynamic, disciplined march of the zigzag . . . the sharp rigid beauty of the zigzag . . . eased to an undulating wave and then to a streaming line."[38] An aesthetic of apparently machine-cut linear patterns enriched the style from the 1929 masterpieces of sculpture at Southern Bell to the abstract foliate incisions on the Evans-Cucich House and the downtown "make-overs" of the mid-thirties. In the end, Deco distinguished itself from other modern styles essentially by its application of setback profile and surface appliqué to architectural form.

AT LEFT: *Deco ornament, 84 Luckie Street (Herrin's Restaurant), facade remodeling by Dillon and Lewis, 1935 (photo by Robert M. Craig)*

CHAPTER 3

The Yaarab Temple:
A Fox in Sheik's Clothing

Even the theater is a "show" without regard to the picture or stage production.

THE CITY BUILDER, APRIL 1930

THE "FABULOUS" FOX THEATRE is Atlanta's premier monument of the Deco era. While stylistically not Art Deco, the theater shares with Art Deco-styled theaters (such as the famed Paramount by Miller and Plueger in Oakland, California, 1931) a lavish display of ornament, a coloristic cosmetic of surface effects, and an appeal to the senses that was essentially populist. It has been described as a "beautifully outlandish, opulent, grandiose monument to the heady excesses of the pre-crash 1920s . . . a masterpiece of trompe l'oeil . . . [which] retained a subtlety of style and a sense of tastefulness."[1] It is, in a word, unique.

The Fox Theatre is a historicist landmark from a populist, progressive, "Deco" era. The Deco style, itself eclectic, was finding design inspiration and ornamental motifs from sources beyond traditional classicism: in Mayan relief decoration, Egyptian friezes, and Mediterranean foliate patterns and abstractions. With this broader range of revivalistic models, the 1920s frenzy for a more exotic historicism, especially in movie palaces, was influencing the designing of Mayan Revival, Aztec, Chinese, Spanish Colonial, and Mission styles; Spanish Renaissance and Baroque revivals; and even native "Apache-styled" theaters.[2] In this company the Atlanta Fox was fashionably dressed for the occasion of stepping out for an evening of culture or entertainment.

If Deco-*styled* movie houses appeared

Architect's drawing, auditorium, Fox Theatre, Marye, Alger, and Vinour, 1925-26 (courtesy of Fox Theatre)

more chic, the Fox was by no means diffident in its architectural makeup and appointments. It was as exotic as Nefertiti, as romantic as Valentino playing "The Sheik" of Araby, as grand and colorful as a Cecil B. DeMille historic production in celluloid.

Art Deco was a stylish style, a style of style, and frequently involved appliqué. If it is anything, the Fox Theatre is likewise a work of style achieved through appliqué. It is Atlanta's ultimate masterpiece of cosmetic architecture. Its rambling structural

FACING PAGE: Yaarab Temple (Fox Theatre), Ponce de Leon Avenue (temple) entrance, Marye, Alger, and Vinour, 1929 (photo courtesy of Fox Theatre)

63

Fox Theatre, Peachtree Street (right) and Ponce de Leon Avenue (left) corner, Marye, Alger, and Vinour, 1929 (photo courtesy of Fox Theatre)

Auditorium, Fox Theatre, Marye, Alger, and Vinour, 1929 (photo by Robert M. Craig)

steel frame appeared to observers, during its late-1920s construction, much like any other engineered large structure of its day: unclothed architectural bones awaiting a skin of as yet undisclosed character. But soon, walls encased the building in striped cream and buff brickwork accented with patterns and limestone trim. Rooftop projections extended skyward to achieve an increasingly romantic silhouette of parapets, small towers, a minaret, and a huge onion dome with patterned copper roof. The modern steel frame was veiled in Eastern dress, draped in architectural robes to create an exotic vision of the Arabian Nights. Interior engineering was also veiled: practical functioning systems, such as heat and air vents, were hidden behind ornate grills; organ pipes in the auditorium disappeared behind "royal box" screens; broom closets and telephone booths were encased in a textured,

stoney plaster; and walls, windows, and doors were accented with bronze hardware, exotic wall lights, and colorfully painted trim.

But the cosmetic face-lift was not intended to display a stylish up-to-date fashion so much as to evoke a fanciful dream imagery of distant times and places. Its decorative and formal models were historic, not modern. The Fox originated as the Yaarab Temple of the Ancient Order of the Nobles of the Mystic Shrine, a mosque headquarters for 5,000 "Shriners" who since 1916 had planned to erect such a building "as a contribution to the civic growth of the Gate City of the South."[3] In 1918, 851 Shrine initiates made a pilgrimage to the Holy City of Mecca and returned to Atlanta inspired to begin their task of planning for the mosque.

Several additional events set the stage for the stylistic choice and architectural charac-

ter of the future Fox Theatre. In 1922, the same year the Shriners acquired their future building site on Peachtree Street at Ponce de Leon, an extraordinary discovery was made in the Valley of the Kings in Egypt. The English archaeologist Howard Carter unearthed an ancient mortuary site, undefiled by previous grave robbers, and opened the tomb of the young pharaoh, Tutankhamen, filled with ancient treasures. The find fascinated the public and influenced designers who saw in the objets d'art and painted images a rich vocabulary of potential contemporary use.

"A frenzy of Egyptomania" resulted. Apartment buildings, commercial retail stores, institutional buildings, and movie theaters began to form their facades as great pylon gateways with cavetto moldings-accented with scarabs and papyrus leaves. Egyptian ornament, pharaonic profiles,

Yaarab Temple (Fox Theatre), Ponce de Leon Avenue (temple) entrance with shops, Marye, Alger, and Vinour, 1929 (photo courtesy of Fox Theatre)

Egyptian Ballroom, Fox Theatre, Marye, Alger, and Vinour, 1929 (photos by Robert M. Craig)

and bud and bell columns enriched an exotic revivalistic architecture across the United States and turned artistic eyes beyond European capitals to the eastern Mediterranean. Grauman's Egyptian Theater (1,800 seats) was built by Meyer and Holler in Hollywood in 1922, the year of the King Tut discovery and five years before

Grauman's more famous Chinese Theater (1927; 2,258 seats) in Hollywood by the same architects. An extraordinary facade of four colossal Egyptian columns appeared in Peery's Egyptian Theatre (1924; 1,500 seats) by Hodgson and McClanahan in Ogden, Utah. Throughout the late 1920s, "Eastern" architectural dress appeared on a range of buildings across North America. Two of the best examples were Morgan, Walls, and Cle-ments' extravagant Assyrian palace built as the headquarters for the Samson Tyre and Rubber Company in Los Angeles in 1929, and the City Hall and government center of Opa-Locka, Florida. The latter was styled as an Arabian vision of minarets and

AT RIGHT: Restoration of King Solomon's Temple, Helmle and Corbett (Hugh Ferriss rendering), proposed for Philadelphia Exposition, Forty-first Annual Exhibition, Architectural League of New York, published in **American Architect** *(February 20, 1926). (Courtesy, Architectural Record, incorporating* **American Architect** *February 20, 1926 [129, no. 2491], copyright 1926 by McGraw-Hill, Inc. All rights reserved. Reproduced with the permission of the publisher.)*

Winning competition design, Yaarab Temple (Fox Theatre), Marye, Alger, and Vinour, 1925-26 (courtesy of Fox Theatre)

mosque domes and would be the only such work of the period[4] in the South to rival the Fox Theatre's Islamic splendor.

About 1925 the architectural firm of Helmle and Corbett produced and published colorful renderings of a restoration of King Solomon's Temple and Citadel. The architect hoped to build a full-scale replica (never executed) at the 1926 Sesquicentennial Exhibition in Philadelphia,[5] but the renderings were enough to inspire Shriners already inclined toward eastern Mediterranean styles. A vast Shrine Civic Auditorium in Los Angeles was built in 1925-26 "with a Moorish tinge" and in 1928 Hugh Davies built in the same city Angeles Abbey, an exotic mausoleum "of the Islamic revival inspired by the Hollywood stage set."[6] In Atlanta, by 1925, the Shriners were boasting that their Yaarab Temple auditorium would "out-Baghdad Baghdad."[7] That same year a building fund was inaugurated, and a competition held for the Yaarab headquarters. Six of Atlanta's best architectural firms entered with Marye, Alger, and Vinour selected as winning designers, having produced a scheme "of pure Mohammedan style."[8] The architects were best known for the design by Marye of Atlanta's famed Terminal Station in 1905; the firm would follow their success at the Fox by building the city's first Modernistic skyscraper, the Southern Bell Building (1929-30).[9]

The extravagant decorative schemes for the Yaarab Temple ran beyond budget from the start, and the entire project was soon threatened. One of the great moguls of the motion picture industry, William Fox, soon came to the rescue. Fox was building movie palaces in Detroit (1928), Brooklyn (1928), San Francisco (1929), and St. Louis (1929),[10] the latter an extravaganza styled in "Cambodian Baroque" and unsurpassed. Fox saw Atlanta as a potential Southeastern jewel in his crown of magnificent movie palaces located nationwide. He arranged with the Temple trustees to guarantee a $3 million, twenty-one-year lease, which would ensure the mosque's completion and would project an ongoing income for the complex. An additional $1.5 million bond issue helped to offset cost overruns, and on Christmas Day 1929 (just months after the great "Black Tuesday" stock-market crash), the Fox Theatre opened. Two days later the Yaarab Temple conducted its first business meeting in the lounge of the Shrine Mosque and initiated its new Shriners on New Year's Eve.

On opening day, the first show at 1:15 filled the 4,504 seats of the auditorium. It was a gala event "such as no perfervid theater-goer could be content to miss," noted _The Atlanta Journal._ The program was opened by an informal fugue on the "Mighty Mo," the auditorium's grand theater organ of 3,622 pipes extending as high as thirty-two feet behind the camouflaging Near-Eastern grills of the balconies flanking the proscenium. Built by the M. P. Moller Company of Hagerstown, Maryland, "opus 5566" was an instrument of 4 keyboards, 376 stops, and 42 ranks. The great organ would provide the prelude to feature films during the golden age of Hollywood and the heyday of the Fox as a movie palace.[11]

Harold B. Franklin, president of Fox West Coast Theatres, in a "screen trailer" (short film) dedicated the theater to Atlanta and to the Southeast, perhaps never dreaming the extent to which the building would become endeared in the hearts of the citizenry. A sound cartoon of "Steamboat Willie" followed with no one in the audience, likely, realizing he had seen the premiere film of the most famous rodent in history, Mickey Mouse. And then the house lights dimmed. Within the surrounding walls of an Arabian city, under a vaulted canopy reaching above the balcony, and below the night sky accented with twinkling lights and wispy clouds, the audience awaited while the organ improvised some mood-transferring notes. In a "triumphal return to the theatrical life of the city," conductor Enrico Leide raised his baton before the assembled orchestra and chorus, spotlights pierced the mysterious atmosphere, and the "graduation processional" cadences of Edward Elgar's "Pomp and Circumstance" began majestically to fill the hall. To this "tune," singers pronounced a musical approbation on "This Shrine of Beauty," in lyrics authored by Ernest Rogers,

Winning competition design, Yaarab Temple (Fox Theatre), Marye, Alger, and Vinour, 1925-26 (courtesy of Fox Theatre)

who the following day would review the whole event in the pages of *The Atlanta Journal.*

A newsreel followed, and if post-Crash economic news continued to be dismal, the audience seemed not to care, for within minutes the master of ceremonies, Don Wilkins, was leading the audience in song. Lilting notes of "Let Me Call You Sweetheart" and "Singing in the Rain" by a chorus of over 4,500 Fox Theatre patrons reverberated throughout the auditorium, and, "believe it or not, the audience sang like they enjoyed it."

The Fanchon and Marco production company, which would present extravagant stage revues at the Atlanta Fox, the St. Louis Fox, and elsewhere in coming years, offered its first "Fanchon and Marco Idea" called "Beach Nights"—good "flesh and blood entertainment," *The Atlanta Journal* observed, "full of class," and enhanced by Don Wilkins' jazz band. On this stage they would discover they could mount productions of extraordinary breadth, because the Atlanta Fox Theatre offered, according to the Chamber of Commerce, the largest theatrical stage in the world: 125 feet wide from wall to wall (4 feet wider than New York's Roxy Theater,[12] 1927, by W. W. Ahlschlager) and 37

70

feet deep. The performance space was framed by an 80-foot-high proscenium arch designed to appear, from the audience's perspective, as a vast masonry bridge lighted by ancient street posts silhouetted against the night sky.

The feature film followed: George O'Brian, Helen Chandler, and William Janney starring in *Salute*, about the army and navy academies. In addition, "several high-key observations which caught the popular fancy" were "kicked in" by "that droll-colored [*sic*] man, Stepin Fetchit."[13] All this entertainment cost adults 60 cents and children 20 cents (35 cents and 15 cents for matinees) with no seats reserved and only the loge requiring an additional 15 cents above the adult price.

The real show, in many ways, was architectural. Ollivier J. Vinour, born in France and educated at the Ecole des Beaux-Arts, was project designer for the building. Beaux-

Arts architects relied on historic models for "authority" and frequently gathered extraordinary libraries of books and journals for source materials. Architects also put together photographic albums and sketchbooks from travels, and amassed from various sources scrapbooks that could serve as reference for formal details, ornament, profiles, window or door designs, furnishings, etc.[14] For the Shrine Mosque and Fox Theatre, Vinour relied on picture books of Egypt, Nubia, and the Holy Land (see colorplate) and a collection of fifty picture postcards obtained from a friend following a grand tour of the Middle East. The result was an eclectic, architectonic collage of borrowed elements from Arabia, India, Turkey, Persia, and Morocco as well as from Egypt and Nubia.[15]

The building's exterior was dominated by a pattern of horizontal stripes, which blanketed the structure in tan and cream

Grand Salon, Fox Theatre, Marye, Alger, and Vinour, 1929 (photo by Robert M. Craig)

71

brickwork and which was punctuated by an extraordinary array of arched openings, corbeled balconies, and parapets. Lancets, arrow-slit openings, four-centered arches, and horseshoe and ogee arches perforated the brick surfaces, providing dramatic accents of shadow and outline across the broad masonry walls. Lace-patterned spandrels, cushion capitals, Syrian Romanesque foliate capitals, exterior staircases, and balcony balustrades provided additional decorative focus. Skyline minarets echoing prayer towers of Islamic mosques enriched the roof profile and accented the corner of the vast theater building as well as its east facade and marquee. The great copper dome of the south (Ponce de Leon Avenue) facade, originally intended to mark the main entrance, was ribbed and ornamented with Eastern crosses and an Islamic crescent as finial.

Peachtree Street, however, was Atlanta's principal avenue, and William Fox established his theater marquee there, at the opening of a vast 140-foot arcade offering primary access to the theater. This reorientation resulted in a sequence of spaces similar to the St. Louis Fox Theater where moviegoers entered from Grand Boulevard (Mid-Town St. Louis's great theater street), through an enclosed vestibule, into a huge Southeast Asian temple interior where popcorn and drinks were sold in exotic splendor during intermission. Atlanta's entry arcade (see colorplate), with low compartmentalized ceiling enriched with stencil and gilt, was open to the street (the climate allowed it) with doors leading into the theater positioned deep within the tunnel space.

In the Fox theaters nationally, grand staircases linked these public entry spaces to imaginative and romantic mezzanines. The San Francisco Fox focused on an operatic Beaux-Arts Classical, neo-Baroque staircase. In St. Louis, a grand staircase extended between flanking rampant beasts, while seated buddhas peered out from the shadows of gigantic imperial red Oriental columns. In Atlanta a staircase at either end of an expansive foyer formed walls and upper-level colonnades to enclose a balconied court visible

AT LEFT: *Ponce de Leon Avenue entry, Fox Theatre, Marye, Alger, and Vinour, 1929 (photo from Robert M. Craig Collection, Atlanta History Center)*

FACING PAGE TOP: *Balcony exits and fire stairs, Ponce de Leon Avenue elevation, Fox Theatre, Marye, Alger, and Vinour, 1929 (photo by Robert M. Craig)*

FACING PAGE MIDDLE: *Ponce de Leon Avenue entry arch decorations, Fox Theatre, Marye, Alger, and Vinour, 1929 (photo by Robert M. Craig)*

FACING PAGE BOTTOM: *Balcony, Apartment, Fox Theatre, Marye, Alger, and Vinour, 1929 (photo by Robert M. Craig)*

from the mezzanine. Patrons looked from the residential balcony openings of an Old Cairo palace at a canopy-framed Arabian landscape painted on the wall beyond. Magnificent thrones and sofas furnished these major foyer spaces of the Fox theaters, with each turn of a corner or staircase landing offering additional surprises and evocative vantage points for inquisitive visitors. In Atlanta, for example, behind the dress circle, patrons find

73

Peachtree Street entry, Fox Theatre, Marye, Alger, and Vinour, 1929 (photo by Robert M. Craig)

The designers of the Atlanta Fox auditorium created a fanciful plaster city of Arabia, sufficiently monumental in scale to evoke the feeling that patrons had gathered on a clear starlit night in the courtyard of a turreted and crenellated walled fortress (see colorplate). From the rear of the balcony extended a billowing canvas tent of striped pattern (actually both sky and canopy are cement vaults suspended from steel crossbeams and reinforced with steel rods). The sky featured ninety-six stars formed of eleven-watt bulbs positioned above two-inch crystals to achieve a twinkling effect of soft stellar highlights.

A Junior Brenograph projected slowly moving clouds across the sky. Its disc regulated by a timer ensured a full revolution in one hour and forty-five minutes. In addition, a Master Brenograph, employing different slides, could change the weather nightly: fog, snow, rain, and with additional circuits engaged, a range of solar effects. The sun machine projected an impression of a sunrise, a "faint pinkish blue glow in the top left rear level" of the auditorium; the rising sun slowly moved toward a "brilliant high noon" above the center seats; and it concluded five minutes later with a sunset on the right side of the proscenium bridge. While the solar show blew its circuitry after only a few years of operation, it was reinstated in the 1970s after nearly forty years of disuse.[16]

It was such visual illusions that prompted these movie palaces to be called "atmospheric" theaters. The artificial effects, achieved by light, surface treatments, and various cosmetic appliqués, prompt one to see the Fox as a landmark of Deco-era artificial artistry.

In addition to public vestibule and reception spaces, intermission lounges, and the auditorium, the Fox offered patrons exotic historic imagery within smoking lounges of the rest rooms at both mezzanine and lower levels, the latter serving the orchestra patrons. The Ladies' Lower Lounge, with its Moorish accents, was dimly lighted by floor and table lights, by recessed ceiling lighting, and by a faceted (Deco zigzag) chandelier. Islamic grill windows and a brightly stenciled

a series of transverse arches vaulting a dimly lighted tunnel that serves as a romantic and mysterious dress-circle promenade.

The loge, dress circle, and balcony seats of the theater auditorium also followed virtually identical plans in both St. Louis and Atlanta, offering the same seating capacity in "atmospheric" spaces of entirely different style. St. Louis's auditorium was flanked by lions and fanciful beasts, wall reliefs of face masks, a magnificent chandelier, and huge Oriental red columns first seen in the hall downstairs. The whole created an ambiance reminiscent of imperial China or Angkor Wat. Atlanta, on the other hand, was a Fox dressed in sheik's clothing.

Men's Lower Lounge, Fox Theatre, Marye, Alger, and Vinour, 1929 (photo courtesy of Fox Theatre)

keyhole doorway suggested Middle-East sources. The Men's Lower Lounge, however, was more explicitly neo-Egyptian, stenciled in friezes and furnished with tables and chairs decorated with winged scarabs. Both the scarab and a stylized falcon symbolized the Egyptian sun god, Osiris, suggesting a mystical connection of the Fox not to Mohammed but to the boy Pharaoh Tutankhamen or Queen Nefertiti. Lighting within a zigzag wall niche reintroduced a certain Deco overtone of setback profiles (see colorplate).

Lounges at mezzanine level, in contrast with the rest rooms downstairs, reversed the stylistic character for each sex, giving patrons the choice of resting in lounges inspired by either the Nile or the Euphrates. The Men's Mezzanine Lounge (see colorplate), like the Ladies' Lounge downstairs, was more Persian than Egyptian with stoney transverse arches and exposed ceiling beams (both plaster), exotic hanging lights, baronial hooded fireplace with tiled hearth, and colorful ceramic wall panels and trim. But the Ladies' Mezzanine Lounge (see colorplates),

under the spell of King Tut, most effectively transported patrons back to the Valley of the Kings. In a pair of rooms even more evocative than the Egyptian Men's Lounge downstairs, the Ladies' Lounge summoned forth images of an ancient mastaba, solid and dense in construction and colorful and delicate in ornamental enrichment. Large blocks of stone rose above a stenciled baseboard, and the walls were crowned with cavetto moldings that flared out to provide housing for recessed upper wall lights. The fireplace was framed by fluted columns with papyrus leaf bases and capped by an entablature of colorful accents and cavetto profile whose winged scarab in central position greeted patrons entering the lounge on axis with the fireplace. Furnishings included large funerary urns, lamps with Egyptian decoration, and ornate armchairs, so rich in relief carving and color that they appeared to be small thrones for Queen Nefertiti. Just beyond, an opening in the thick wall led to cosmetic tables and stools with elaborate mirrors, sconces, and delicate metal mounts. Door hardware, brass escutcheon plates, and

75

signs throughout the theater continued the themes of Egptian and Near-Eastern exoticism. As *The City Builder* noted in April 1930, the "Fox Theatre in [the] Shrine Mosque . . . is a 'show' without regard to the picture or stage production."[17]

The most monumental Egyptian space within the Fox Theatre complex was built by the Shriners as a Banquet Hall and is today known as the Egyptian Ballroom. Like the rest of the theater, the ballroom in recent years has been completely restored to its original splendor, duplicating hundreds of stencil patterns for ceiling decoration, restoring painted and glazed ornaments, and reinstating original colors (see colorplate). The rejuvenated Fox of today, however, gives little hint of the theater's years of trauma since the days of Fanchon and Marco and the Yaarab Temple headquarters.

The earliest years of the Fox were the years of deepest economic depression in the United States, and although jazz bands, sound movies, and stage productions could provide escape for patrons of the Fox, The Fox Theatre Corporation itself went bankrupt as early as 1932. The Yaarab Temple Building Corporation's investment was lost, and although Loew's Theatre Corporation had been jointly managing the Fox since 1930, that arrangement ended in 1932 and the Fox closed in June. It was the depth of the Great Depression. After efforts in late summer to reopen, the mortgage was finally foreclosed in December, just three years after the jubilant 1929 grand opening. The complex was then auctioned for $75,000 to the Theatre Holding Company, owned by officers of the Yaarab Temple. When this latter entity collapsed, the City of Atlanta took over the complex for nonpayment of taxes.[18]

Egyptian Ballroom, Fox Theatre, Marye, Alger, and Vinour, 1929 (photo by Robert M. Craig)

Fox Theatre, Marye, Alger, and Vinour, 1929 (photo by Robert M. Craig)

By 1935 the Fox was again showing movies, but when the 1939 classic *Gone with the Wind* premiered in Atlanta just ten days before the Fox Theatre's tenth anniversary, it would not be the Fox, but the Loew's Grand, which would host the great motion picture event.[19] By World War II, Atlanta was developing a cultural life around Big Band concerts by such greats as Tommy Dorsey, Kay Kyser, and Artie Shaw, and dance music and jazz filled the Peachtree Street theaters, including the Fox. From the late 1940s to the end of the 1960s, New York's Metropolitan Opera Company offered a week of opera in the Fox, continuing "Opera Week" in the Civic Center until the Met's Atlanta visits ended altogether in the early 1980s. But for twenty years after World War II, the Fox was at the center of Atlanta's night life.

During the 1950s, the Fox installed a 35-mm projector and Cinemascope screen (one of the earliest movie theaters in the South to do so) in order to feature the grand motion pictures of the 1950s.[20] But by the early 1970s the film industry was consciously dealing lethal blows to larger downtown theaters nationwide by promoting multiple suburban-mall, black-box movie houses. By

1974 the Fox, the grandest of Atlanta's urban theaters, appeared doomed. Plans were announced to demolish the entire theater/ballroom/retail complex to make way for a midtown headquarters for Southern Bell. A nonprofit organization, Atlanta Landmarks, Inc., was soon formed and initiated a "Save the Fox" campaign. At age forty-five, the building was placed on the National Register of Historic Places, despite its not yet being a half-century old (a normal prerequisite for such listing). Within two years, the Fox Theatre was designated a National Historic Landmark.

But the key to its salvation would not be just the recognition of the Fox Theatre's historic and cultural significance, for without a viable economic base, no plaque could prevent its demolition. Atlanta Landmarks took out a three-year, $1.8 million loan in 1975, which it was able to repay six months early, thanks to an extraordinary series of contributions, fund raisers, grants, and celebrity benefits. By the time the theater celebrated its own fiftieth anniversary in 1979, the Fox had been saved and the theater has made profits every year since.[21]

By 1986 three theaters nationally were

competing for honors as the "best large venue for U.S. touring shows," and two were Fox theaters, Atlanta's and St. Louis's. The third was Radio City Music Hall (1932 by Donald Deskey) in New York. In 1988, Atlanta captured the honors when it was recognized as the number-one grossing theater of its class[22] in the country. The Atlanta Fox had "the most events, the greatest box office receipts, and the highest attendance in the U.S." The following year, when *Les Misérables* ran for three weeks in the Atlanta Fox, the musical broke all U.S. box-office records.[23] The clever Fox had emerged from its lair to snare with unsurpassed aplomb the great prize: it had become the ultimate people's palace.

Today, the Fox is the focal point of a rejuvenated historic district including William Stoddart's Ponce de Leon Hotel (1912-13) and the same architect's Georgian Terrace Hotel (1910-11), the latter recently renovated with a new addition by Smallwood, Reynolds, Stewart, Stewart, and Associates (1989-91). A new Yaarab Temple was built just down the street (Ponce de Leon Avenue) in 1963-65, a faint echo of the visionary Shriners colossus of 1929, but still Near Eastern in style. Remarkably, considering years of bankruptcy, foreclosure, and threatened demolition, the Great Mosque and Fabulous Fox have survived. The Fox preens today in the splendor it displayed when it opened to a chorus line of Fanchon and Marco dancers. If historic Peachtree Street, where Margaret Mitchell wrote her classic novel of the Old South, conjures in our imaginations visions of a mythic Atlanta of peach blossoms and horse-drawn carriages, at least for one short block north of Ponce de Leon, the ride along Peachtree is taken on a magic carpet.

CHAPTER 4

Modern Classic and the New Deal

Franklin D. Roosevelt has made Cheops, Pericles . . . and Peter the Great look like a club of birdhouse-builders. . . . For one Parthenon, [the PWA] has reared thousands of glistening city halls, courthouses, post offices, school houses . . .

LIFE MAGAZINE, 1940

There are cycles in architecture, but people always return to the classics.

LEWIS E. CROOK, JR.

[Good modern design requires] a breaking away from the old architecture [and] a loyalty to it . . . the Moderne traditionalized, the Traditional modernized.

THE FEDERAL ARCHITECT, 1930

THE GRAND OPENING of the extravagant Atlanta Fox Theatre just weeks after the 1929 stock-market crash, and the completion of the exuberant Deco-Gothic City Hall a few weeks after that, offered dramatic contrasts with the realities of the early months of the Great Depression. Throughout the post-Crash years of the Hoover administration, monetary deflation, financial insecurity both at home and abroad, rising unemployment, factory closings and bank failures, and growing economic hardship found aesthetic expression in an increasingly ascetic and restrained architectural style associated with the 1930s.

Identified generally as "Depression Modern," a more economic and sparing imagery in the 1930s reduced elaborate Art Deco polychromatic patterns to simpler "Modernistic" block forms, more monumental but also more limited in their bas-reliefs. Horizontal enrichments were stretched and streamlined into "lines of least resistance," marking a phase of contemporary "Moderne" discussed in the following volume.

The effects both of thirties economies and of increasingly simpler modern aesthetic tendencies were also felt within traditional architectural styles. The grandiloquent Beaux-Arts Classicism of the Edwardian era became by the second quarter-century the "elementarism" of a modern classicism. This was evidenced in projects ranging from English architect Edwin Lutyens' 1920s war memorials and New Delhi Viceroy's House to Paul Cret's restrained classicism in 1930s Washington, D.C. or at the Chicago Century of Progress Exposition in 1933-34, where he served as design consultant.

The simpler classicism, which has been interpreted as a traditional architecture "modernized," was particularly manifested in official governmental architecture from the thirties through the fifties. The tendency has prompted historians to invent such stylistic terms as "PWA Classic" (or even "WPA Classic"), "Classical Moderne," and "Modern Classic."[1] Such terms, of course, have been linked to the New Deal, although the tendencies toward austerity and simplicity,

ABOVE: *Federal Post Office Building, A. Ten Eyck Brown (Alfredo Barili, Jr., and J. W. Humphreys, associates; James Wetmore, supervising architect), 1931-33 (photo by Robert M. Craig)*

State Health Building, A. Thomas Bradbury, 1958 (photo by Robert M. Craig)

Roosevelt High School (formerly Girls' High School, now The Roosevelt), Edwards and Sayward
(A. Ten Eyck Brown, supervising architect), 1924 (photo by Robert M. Craig)

ABOVE: *United Motors Service Building, A. Ten Eyck Brown, 1920 (photo by Robert M. Craig)*

BELOW: *Lobby directory, William-Oliver Building, Pringle and Smith, 1930 (photo by Robert M. Craig)*

Architect's presentation drawing, Rhodes-Haverty Building, Pringle and Smith, 1929 (photo by Robert M. Craig, courtesy of Henry Howard Smith, Architect)

Radiator grill, lobby, William-Oliver Building, Pringle and Smith, 1930 (photo by Robert M. Craig)

Lobby stair balustrade, William-Oliver Building, Pringle and Smith, 1930 (photo by Robert M. Craig)

Lobby cove ornament, William-Oliver Building, Pringle and Smith, 1930 (photo by Robert M. Craig)

Detail, light, W. W. Orr Building, Pringle and Smith, 1930 (photo by Robert M. Craig)

Light, Southern Bell Telephone Company Building, Marye, Alger, and Vinour, 1929 (photo by Robert M. Craig)

Lobby staircase, City Hall, G. Lloyd Preacher, 1929-30 (photo by Robert M. Craig)

Frieze ornament, Southern Bell Telephone Company Building, Marye, Alger, and Vinour, 1929 (photo by Robert M. Craig)

Lobby, City Hall, G. Lloyd Preacher, 1929-30 (photo by Robert M. Craig)

ABOVE: *Terra-cotta capital ornament, Troy Peerless Laundry Building, Isaac Moscowitz, 1928-29 (photo by Robert M. Craig)*

BELOW: *Terra-cotta ornament, C. E. Freeman Ford Agency, G. Lloyd Preacher, 1930 (photo by Robert M. Craig)*

A Street in Old Cairo, *from a mid-nineteenth-century collection of drawings of Egypt and Nubia by David Roberts (courtesy of Georgia Tech Architecture Library)*

Entry arcade, Fox Theatre, Marye, Alger, and Vinour, 1929 (photo by Robert M. Craig)

Auditorium, Fox Theatre, Marye, Alger, and Vinour, 1929 (photo by Robert M. Craig)

Men's Lower Lounge, Fox Theatre, Marye, Alger, and Vinour, 1929 (photo by Robert M. Craig)

Men's Mezzanine Lounge, Fox Theatre, Marye, Alger, and Vinour, 1929 (photo by Robert M. Craig)

Egyptian Ballroom, Fox Theatre, Marye, Alger, and Vinour, 1929 (photo by Robert M. Craig)

Ladies' Mezzanine Lounge, Fox Theatre, Marye, Alger, and Vinour, 1929 (photo by Robert M. Craig)

ABOVE: *Ladies' Mezzanine Lounge, Fox Theatre, Marye, Alger, and Vinour, 1929 (photo by Robert M. Craig)*

BELOW: *Federal Post Office Building, A. Ten Eyck Brown (Alfredo Barili, Jr., and J. W. Humphreys, associates; James Wetmore, supervising architect), 1931-33 (photo by Robert M. Craig)*

AT LEFT: *Gymnasium and Auditorium, Georgia Tech, Bush-Brown and Gailey, 1936-37 (PWA/WPA project, razed 1994) (photo by Robert M. Craig)*

Citizens and Southern Bank, Hentz, Adler and Shutze, 1920s, covered in 1949 by new metal-panel facade of Citizens Jewelry Company expansion (photo by Robert M. Craig)

Alumni Hall, Georgia State University, new facade, Robert and Co., 1943 (from Lake County [IL] Museum/Curt Teich Postcard Archives, courtesy of the Atlanta History Center)

appearing even before Franklin Delano Roosevelt's administration, may suggest more broadly a coming together of traditional and modern aesthetics. Most certainly, the predilection of federal, state, and to a lesser degree municipal governmental architecture to employ classical forms is reflected in the Modern Classic style; but the minimal elaboration of thirties Modern Classicism is also a reflection of the constraints and economies of a period of national depression. As the country slipped deeper into the Great De-

pression from early 1930 to early 1933, late-twenties decorative excess—from the polychromatic Deco to the exotic historicism of the Fox—was stripped away to form the restrained monumental Deco and Modern Classic of the 1930s. The 1930-33 work in Atlanta by A. Ten Eyck Brown reflected this tendency.

Three projects designed by A. Ten Eyck Brown opened the new decade on a self-evidently restrained note. The Volunteer State Life Building, designed in association with

Volunteer State Life Building, A. Ten Eyck Brown (Alfredo Barili, Jr., associate), 1931 (courtesy of the Atlanta History Center)

Alfredo Barili, Jr., was built in 1931 along the full block of Luckie Street between Forsyth and Broad. Its lower two floors were surfaced in glazed, black brick, and storefront windows and the Luckie Street entry door enframement were aluminum. Five middle-level floors composed a facade of undefiled Chicago Style commercial frame, while the top two floors were adorned with classic pilasters topped by circular medallions and a delicate horizontal relief band incised across the top. The tripartite elevation was plain, expressive of its structural frame, and delicately neoclassical. It was an economic design of moderation rather than exuberance, of the early thirties rather than the late twenties.

Brown also designed the "Ten Pryor Street Building" or Thornton Building,[2] constructed from 1930 to 1932. Commissioned by Albert E. Thornton to replace a block of buildings erected in the 1870s by his grandfather, Gen. Alfred Austell, the Thornton

Building reflected in its restrained form the unprecedented national economic depression of the years of its construction. It presented its only color-enriched ornament at ground level, built upper floors with bare-bones minimalism, and abandoned entirely the projected top four stories of its original design. Completed in 1932, its stripped aesthetic communicated that 1932 (and the early months of 1933 before Roosevelt's inauguration) were the deepest moments of the Great Depression.

From the start Brown envisioned a starkly simple framework encased in limestone without elaborate moldings, stringcourses, or crowning cornice. The flat roof and smooth monochromatic planarity of the facing material were relieved only by the black and green Tinus marble of the storefront bases and the brass window and door frames at ground level. Brass elevators enriched the lobbies. But as evidenced at the

Thornton Building, A. Ten Eyck Brown, 1930-32 (photo by Robert M. Craig)

Volunteer Building, a minimal Modern Classic was suggested by fluted pilasters on exterior facades and the horizontal relief bands and geometric patterns at different levels on the street elevations. The flexibility of interior spaces, able to be subdivided "scientifically and efficiently [to] arrange floor space," was considered "ultramodern" at the time the building opened. Most of all, it was the stark simplicity of the exterior forms that reflected the contemporary stylistic tendencies in depression-era modern architecture.

Brown's third built work of the period was Atlanta's largest construction project of the early 1930s, and was sponsored by the federal government. The Federal Post Office Building, now the Martin Luther King, Jr. Federal Building, was erected opposite Terminal Station to provide Atlanta's main sorting and distribution center for both the city and the Southeast. The new Post Office was a $3 million project constructed in steel and reinforced concrete and surfaced in stone and terra-cotta above a granite base. Interior finish included "first class durable materials with marble used in the main lobbies and stairs, terrazza [*sic*] floors and wainscots in the office corridors, metal lobby screen, [and] modern mechanical equipment."[3]

As a federal project, the building reflected a governmental classical style, but as *The City Builder* noted, "the enormous scale of this structure has necessitated the simplification of the usual classic characteristics of government building...." Instead of a more extravagant Beaux-Arts Classical federal building, as John Knox Taylor had provided Atlanta in 1908-11 for its Renaissance Revival-styled Old Post Office, the new Post Office would be a "Modern Classic" work of restrained low relief and simple profile. Indeed, a theatrical monumentality was achieved by the scale of the building's substantial setback forms (see colorplate),

ABOVE: *Federal Post Office Building, A. Ten Eyck Brown (Alfredo Barili, Jr., and J. W. Humphreys, associates; James Wetmore, supervising architect), 1931-33 (photo by Robert M. Craig)*

AT RIGHT: *Entry ornament, Federal Post Office Building, A. Ten Eyck Brown (Alfredo Barili, Jr., and J. W. Humphreys, associates; James Wetmore, supervising architect), 1931-33 (photo by Robert M. Craig)*

recalling Hugh Ferriss's *Metropolis* charcoal sketches of setback towers and weighty masses set in dramatic shadow and mysterious light (see Hugh Ferriss sketch, page 37).

The new Post Office was not an "academic" public building of the Beaux-Arts tradition profusely enriched with figural sculpture, painted murals, and elaborate decoration. Ornament played a role, but it appeared machine cut and modern. Doors were decorated with Deco sunbursts, sharp-edged eagles, postal-service emblems, and low-relief friezes. It was the drama of the architectural forms that was most striking. As a contemporary writer noted when construction got under way, "the securing of a monumental design has been accomplished in outline and profile by carefully studied set backs and alternating plain and pierced surfaces together with the prospective use of massive and durable materials. . . ."[4] Completed on the eve of the New Deal, the new Federal Post Office embodied features that extend beyond a simplified modern Deco to embrace a new thirties style of government-sponsored Modern Classic.

The Atlanta Federal Post Office is a landmark of the city's Deco-to-Modern era and

one of the region's most significant public works in the Modern Classic style. Art Deco historian Eva Weber describes the Modern Classic (calling it classical moderne) in terms applicable to the 1933 Atlanta Post Office: it is "a more conservative style, blending a simplified and monumental modern neo-classicism with a more austere form of geometric and stylized relief sculpture and other ornament. . . ."[5] Such descriptions were found to apply to several projects during the New Deal years to follow.

Two years after the Federal Post Office was completed in Atlanta, the nearby town of Decatur, Georgia, erected a small U.S.

ABOVE: *Detail, light, Federal Post Office Building, A. Ten Eyck Brown (Alfredo Barili, Jr., and J. W. Humphreys, associates; James Wetmore, supervising architect), 1931-33 (photo by Robert M. Craig)*

AT LEFT: *U.S. Post Office and Federal Building, Decatur, Georgia, 1935 (photo by Robert M. Craig)*

Police Station and Jail, Burge and Stevens, 1934-35 (photo by Robert M. Craig)

Police Station and Jail, Burge and Stevens, 1934-35 (photo by Robert M. Craig)

Post Office and Federal Building in a restrained classical style. The flat-roofed building's smooth exterior presented a sharp-edged rectangle of extreme austerity, relieved only by zigzag profiles as the wall stepped into the centrally placed entry door and balancing windows. Above each runs a continuous band of Greek frets that wraps the building in an effort to suggest an attic level on the upper facade. Dating from 1935, Decatur's Federal Building is a project of the New Deal's "recovery" years, a federal project of clear classical expression but still constrained by the economies of the era.

The firm of Burge and Stevens combined the simple forms and monumental scale of a weighty Modern Classicism in the Atlanta Police Station and Jail (1934-35), completed soon after Ten Eyck Brown's Atlanta Post Office had established a model for Modernistic design. The Police Station and Jail composed massive blocks of lofty and strong profile in a work whose institutional and fortress character was, as nineteenth-century writer J. C. Loudon might have noted with approval, appropriately intimidating. The twin blocks, indeed, echoed the 1893 Police Station (since

razed) to which it was attached, a massive Victorian Lombardic Romanesque arrangement of brick-and-stone-trim tower set between weighty block wings. Beaux-Arts practitioners would have concluded both buildings had "character."

Burge and Stevens' 1935 penal fortress displayed a rough-hewn primitivism. Its spirit reached back beyond classical history to Paleolithic masons who chipped Cyclopean stone into crude form. Recognizing that one feature of the new Modernistic style is that the building appears to have been cut out of a single block of material, Carol Flores has written of the Atlanta Jail:

> It is easy to imagine a master stonecutter slicing into a block of concrete and lifting out a center section to form the two, massive tower units. With shorter strokes, he creates the setbacks and, finally, incises the two vertical slits on each tower completing his composition. Quickly alternating his master scalpel with precise diagonal shifts, he lightly carves the decorative pattern to finish his scheme.[6]

This Modern Classic is archaic Deco, a design

of unpolished simplicity that achieves its architectonic power through the directness of its forms.

Some commercial architecture of the period adopted this "archaic" Modern Classicism, combining block forms cut in Deco profiles and bas-relief, classic symmetry, and simple detailing. The reduction of ornamental effects encouraged a greater awareness of the role of sound proportions and scale as determinants of the harmony of these facades. The Sharian Building (1946) by Bothwell and Nash and the Rutland Building (1939), both in Decatur, present poised facades of classic tripartite composition, projecting a vertical entry bay forward as a counterpoint to the horizontal lines of fenestration and decorative accents. The Sharian Building layers bands of solid and void and a chevron frieze in a classical arrangement of carefully scaled and balanced elements. At the Rutland, an Egyptian-Deco pylon encases the entry, whose vertical keystone and sunburst above the door are favorite Deco features. Streamlined corners bring a further styling to the building in this synthesis of ancient, Deco, and streamlined elements.

The confident orchestration of such Modernistic elements recalls some of the best elevations of the small hotels, apartments, and commercial buildings of South Miami Beach (but without the recent "Tropical Deco" recoloring). This is especially evident at the Rutland Building, whose streamlined corners and Deco details combine, as they do so often in the Florida work of L. Murray Dixon and Henry Hohauser, to create Modernistic hybrids. Like the Deco-Moderne-Modern ensembles of Hohauser and Dixon, the Sharian and Rutland are completely satisfying syntheses of balanced formal elements of the progressive modern period.

As a stylistic phase of the Deco-to-Modern era, the Modern Classic (without overly explicit classical quotation) brings to institutional and commercial buildings an orderly equipoise, a humanist scale, and a degree of monumentality even in the smallest projects. Such works, in spirit, are related to the noble post office project of A. Ten Eyck

Brown, Atlanta's most monumental institutional landmark of the Modern Classic. Commercial architecture during the period also adopted the more limited vocabulary of Brown's Volunteer and Thornton buildings and found influence both in the rationalist frame of steel or concrete buildings and in the increasingly more reserved Modern Classic of governmental architecture.

An economy of line and decorative detail had already appeared in commercial design during the previous decade when skyscrapers expressed a minimal formal historicism. In 1922 Burge and Stevens erected for Charles F. Palmer a four-story office structure in a simplified Georgian style that remained expressive of its concrete frame. The Palmer Building's brick cladding with limestone trim was resurfaced in 1938 in black and white structural glass to effect a depression-era Modern Classic aesthetic.[7] The following year the firm erected for the same client a twelve-story 101 Marietta Building, an exposed reinforced-concrete structure, in a subdued neo-Gothic style, considered, when built, the largest all-concrete office structure in the Southeast. Neither the Palmer nor 101 Marietta buildings survives, but three restrained office buildings of 1923, the Glenn Building, the Haas-Howell Building, and the Bona Allen Building, are extant. Erected in downtown Atlanta in a simplified style expressive of its structural frame, each is manifestly economical in its imagery. While maintaining a Chicago School compositional organization in their elevations, these buildings avoided the elaborate ornamental cladding of both the Sullivanesque and academic decorative traditions.

In 1928 the firm of Burge and Stevens projected for the first of these, the Glenn Building, a million-dollar addition calling for uniformed attendants servicing a 171-car parking garage of seven floors.[8] A small garage addition was completed with smooth limestone facing matching the original structure, including a delicately ornamented terra-cotta frieze beneath the windows. Piers on the Glenn Building were crowned by stylized Ionic capitals adorned

*Sharian Building,
Decatur, Georgia,
Bothwell and Nash, 1946
(photo by Robert M.
Craig)*

BELOW: *Rutland Building,
Decatur, Georgia, 1939
(photo by Robert M.
Craig)*

in turn by acroterion forms centered in the capital. Above the capitals are discs that some observers suspect may be automobile hubcaps. A reinforced-concrete addition of the same year to the 1912 Southern Railway Offices similarly adorned pier buttresses with stylized floral patterns and thick stamens. Such ornaments serve as transitions from the robust Beaux-Arts Classicism of the academic tradition to the abstractions of a restrained classicism during the thirties.

These works of 1923-28, despite discovered classical detail, remained severe designs of restrained surfaces and straitlaced propriety. Directly expressing their frames, such modern steel towers of the 1920s anticipated the austere style of the 1930s.

A more direct foretaste of the thirties style is provided by the J. P. Allen Building of 1926-27, designed by Thomas Henry Morgan, founding president of the Atlanta Chapter of the AIA. Morgan, Dillon, and Lewis's J. P. Allen Building, like Pringle and Smith's Art Deco Regenstein's Department Store, reflects the shift of business first established on Whitehall Street downtown

(this section is now Peachtree Street South) to a new, northern downtown retail area at present-day Peachtree Center. The J. P. Allen Building was a restrained classical work of Modern Classic ornament and clean limestone surfaces, an early-thirties building aesthetically, but built in the late 1920s.

Especially interesting is the way in which the classic (and Sullivanesque) tripartite elevation of the J. P. Allen storefront is reordered to de-emphasize any suggestion of tallness. Pioneer skyscraper designer Louis Sullivan had organized the street level, offices, and attic (cornice and parapet) of tall buildings as base, shaft, and capital in order

Top Left: *Bona Allen Building, DeFord Smith and John F. Downing, 1923 (photo by Robert M. Craig)*

Top Right: *Glenn Building, Wadley B. Wood, 1923; Parking Annex, Burge and Stevens, 1928 (photo by Robert M. Craig)*

to bring an expressive verticality to the buildings. But here, Morgan substantially projected a continuous cornice with parapet above, and extended horizontally the short two-story middle section of offices above street-level storefronts, each level composed in such a way as to place emphasis on the horizontal rather than the vertical. The regularity and stability of window composition is framed by unbroken horizontal elements of stringcourse, cornice, and shadow. This, along with the planar simplicity of surfaces, anticipates Modern impulses, without yet wholly embracing Modernism's emphasis on functional spaces. Thomas Morgan created in the J. P. Allen Building a work, still, of articulated classical form, not yet Modern volumetric expression; nevertheless, the building offers a precocious synthesis of restrained classical and progressively modern elements, defining its aesthetic as fundamentally Modern Classic.

The J. P. Allen Building was completed about the time European Modernism was just raising its head as an adaptable, international, twentieth-century style based on functionalism rather than historic authority and precedent. The famed Stuttgart Housing Exhibition of 1927 had brought together avant-garde European architects such as Mies van der Rohe, Walter Gropius, Le Corbusier, Bruno Taut, J. J. P. Oud, and others to display starkly modern functionalist designs for housing. Already that year, Richard Neutra had built an apartment building in the new style in Los Angeles and would frame in steel a completely Modern house by 1929. Modernism was ready for importation from Europe, but many traditionalists in America were not yet ready for it.

In 1930 an editorial in *The Federal Architect*[9] described Modern architecture as a germ infecting design through "nose-thumbing at the past." Not dismissing modernism as all bad, the federal architects remained open to a possible synthesis of past and present as a compromise approach. Good modern design, it was felt, required "a breaking away from the old architecture" as well as "a loyalty to it," that is, observed the editorial writer, "the Moderne traditionalized, the Traditional modernized."[10]

Such a synthesis was achieved in the only known large office building designed by the

Atlanta residential firm of Frazier and Bodin, the 1930 Industrial Life and Health Insurance Building. Frazier and Bodin's best known Atlanta work was for the developer and contractor Charles Black, Jr., in the Tuxedo Park area of Buckhead. For a wealthy clientele preferring academic designs, the architects provided Tudor Revival, Neo-Classical, and other eclectic styles for homes constructed throughout the 1930s. In their largest and most public building, however, they turned to the Modern Classic. The Industrial Life and Health Insurance Building, a direct expression of its steel framing, is minimally articulated with classic detailing, including rosettes, dentil moldings, and delicate friezes of almost abstract simplicity. It promotes an image, both traditional and progressive, for an insurance company seeking to be up-to-date.

In Atlanta, the architectural firm of Ivey and Crook crossed this same boundary between traditionalism and a history-informed modern aesthetic. Their Atlanta work dating from the mid-1930s brought a new dimension to the city's Modern Classic aesthetic of the time. The partnership of Ernest Daniel ("Ed") Ivey and Lewis Edmund ("Buck") Crook, Jr., was formed in 1923 and is today best remembered for its traditional neoclassical designs for porticoed and steepled churches, Southern colonial porticoed houses, and elegant college buildings for Emory University. "There are cycles in architecture," wrote Buck Crook, "but people always return to the classics."[11] In commercial architecture Ivey and Crook reflected in a minimal classicism the stylistic trends and economies of form and ornament evidenced in Brown and Barili's work of the early

Modern Classic and the New Deal

Industrial Life and Health Insurance Building, Frazier and Bodin, 1930 (photo by Robert M. Craig)

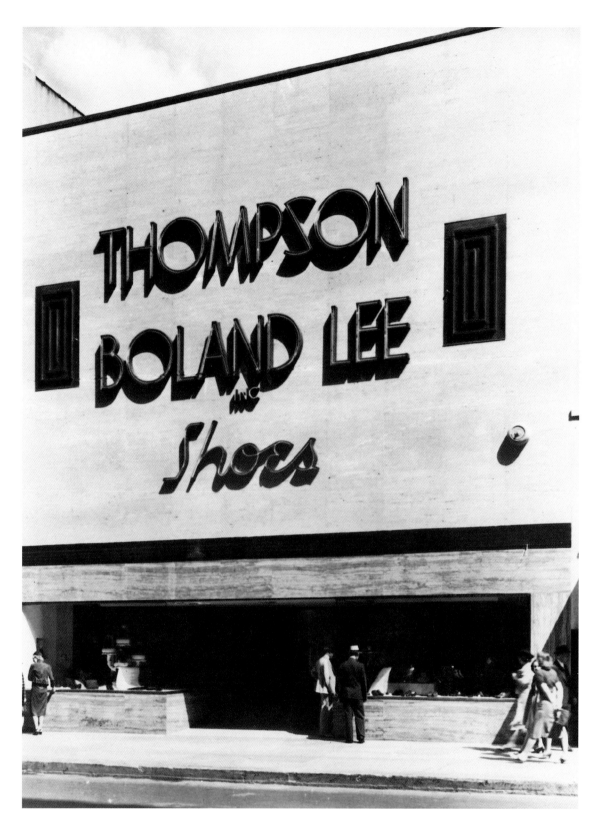

1930s. Like Frazier and Bodin's singular effort, the thirties commercial classicism of
Ivey and Crook had a distinctly modern air.

Three commercial buildings by Ivey and
Crook display the firm's assured familiarity
with classical detail and proportions, applied
to works of such simplicity that their inherent architectural qualities often went unnoticed. The 1939 Peachtree Street shoe store for
Thompson Boland Lee, Inc. converted the
entire facade to a billboard with four-foot lettering and two large flanking panels of con-
centric rectangles transformed from Greek
frets. The ground-level display windows and

recessed entry created a continuous void, cut from the base, which is distinctly modern. A facade of striking simplicity (since altered), Thompson Boland Lee's storefront was a work of careful proportion and scale, distributing elements across an abstract plane whose assured balance was a product of its designer's classical interests.

Such classical inspiration and harmonious and quiet beauty have not always been recognized as meritorious features of the firm's more sparing exercises in neoclassicism. When Rhodes Center (1937-39) was reviewed by the City of Atlanta in recent years for possible historic landmark status, one member of the Zoning Review Board looked with blind eye and numbed mind at Rhodes Center's economic lines and restrained Modern Classicism and saw only ordinary buildings, not architecture; she remarked that she could see the impressive qualities of the exotic Fox Theatre but could not recognize why Rhodes Center should be declared histori-cally significant. Design merit and historic significance, linked only to assertive ornament and flamboyant architectural personality, condemned by default this quiescent roadside complex, and Rhodes Center's reserved elegance and minimal classicism, having failed its rezoning as a historic building, fell before the wrecking ball.[12]

Indeed, Rhodes Center of 1937-39 and the Olympia Building of 1935-36 were significant works of the depression-era Modern Classic style by one of the city's most prominent architectural firms of the day. In particular, Rhodes Center was the city's first suburban shopping and entertainment center, an early commercial strip of retail stores, theater, and restaurant located at the north end of the city's prime "automobile street" of the thirties and forties, Spring Street. The buildings of the center were very plain aesthetically, finding an economy of line appropriate to their late-depression-era construction, and the center turned to classicism as expressive of a refined and simple elegance and beauty. "Eyes which do not see" (looking from the years of the Great Recession) dismissed Rhodes Center as bland and (because it had been left by its owner to deteriorate) ugly. Despite tenants who wished to stay on, the owner razed more than half Rhodes Center in 1992 with no immediate prospects of replacing it with the projected new building argued to be a more economic use of the site.

Rhodes Center was developed by the heirs of the A. G. Rhodes Estate and built in coordinated blocks around three sides of the 1903 baronial mansion, Rhodes Hall.[13] The center included Rhodes Theater, a 1939 movie house earliest to open in the shopping

center, and by 1940 a drugstore, lending library, chiropractor, liquor store, grocer, barber, five-and-dime, and the May Fair Restaurant. No facility for off-street parking was provided; indeed, the horseless carriages positioned themselves "nose in" in front of retail shops like horses at hitching posts along the streets. However, it would only be a matter of months before Briarcliff Plaza, a second shopping center for Atlanta, was constructed with off-street parking, recognized immediately as a vital feature for shopping centers in an increasingly automobile-oriented society.[14]

Rhodes Center was faced in marble and ornamented along the parapet by small triangular pediments with acroterion "ears" derived from ancient Greek temple architecture. Fluted piers served to define these bays as temple fronts, accenting individual rental units at the center or ends of large commercial blocks. A delicate linear band extended across the top of display windows to unify the grouped units of the shopping center. Large plate-glass windows opened the lower facade for commercial display purposes, and the combination of abstract volumes, clean lines, and smooth surfaces declared this neoclassical work to be modern. Rhodes Center's classical features, barely defined by shadow lines, served to compose decorative and formal elements with the utmost restraint. At Atlanta's first shopping center, Ivey and Crook's highly rational classicism displayed itself with a minimalism that was self-consciously progressive.

Ivey and Crook's other major commercial building of the Modern Classic was built in 1935-36 at a prime triangular site at the "Five Points" intersection of Marietta and Peachtree streets. Commissioned by Frank Hawkins, the Olympia Building built its storefronts at sidewalk edge, displaying large shop windows at ground level and smooth, moderately adorned classical surfaces above. Atop second-floor windows were recessed panels with Greek fretwork. The vertical piers between windows were detailed as pilasters, supporting a crowning entablature defined by a band of waves and

Rhodes Center, Ivey and Crook, 1939 (photo by Robert M. Craig, courtesy of Atlanta Urban Design Commission)

Olympia Building, Ivey and Crook, 1935-36 (photo above from Robert M. Craig Collection, Atlanta History Center; at left by Robert M. Craig)

a second band of dentil molding, which wrap around the building. The smooth stone facing was as restrained as other depression-era buildings, but the elegant classical refinements offered hope of a recovery during these New Deal years, when the economy was beginning to show signs of improvement.

A similar repressed Modern Classicism informed a design by Ivey and Crook as late as 1950 in a work not executed until 1961, the Presbyterian Center. A large office block on an extended landscape site, the Presbyterian Center looks to Modern postwar expression of frame and office units in its simple main block, and accents the building with a neoclassical beacon in the spirit of the firm's earlier work during the 1930s.[15]

Presbyterian Center, Ivey and Crook, 1950, 1961-66 (photo by Robert M. Craig)

One of the leading form makers of the Modern Classic style in America was the architect and educator Paul P. Cret of the University of Pennsylvania, whose most notable design in this mode is the Folger Shakespeare Library (1932) in Washington, D.C. Cret, a Beaux-Arts-trained architect, became a prominent mentor for a generation of early modernists. Cret predicted in 1925, as tendencies to a more modern design began to appear internationally, that "a new classicism, achieving beauty through good proportions rather than through the picturesque, will be born."[16] Believing that his Beaux-Arts education contributed artistic qualities to his profession through "proportion . . . ingenuity in planning, adaption to new needs, and refinement in details,"[17] Cret promoted classical values in contemporary architecture. His Folger Shakespeare Library fulfilled the promise of his professed aesthetic intentions, helping to "solidify his position as a champion of principles . . . of mediation between the classical revival gaining ground in the twenties and the irrepressible power of modernism."[18] The library struck a balance between the modern traditionalized and the traditional modernized, and it became one of the most influential designs of its day. In Atlanta it served as a model for Georgia Tech's Heisman Gymnasium and Auditorium Building of 1934-39, the centerpiece of three New Deal projects on campus.[19]

These three buildings lined Third Street at the north end of Grant Field and represented a notable ensemble of CWA (Civil Works Administration), WPA, and PWA projects of the New Deal era, erected between 1934 and 1941. The first building, the Naval Armory, was constructed in 1934-35 on the site of the temporary gymnasium, which had burned in 1931. The Armory was used for forty-five years until its demolition in 1980 to make way for the Edge Intercollegiate Athletic Center. Constructed under the CWA, an agency created by Roosevelt's Federal Emergency Relief Act of May 1933, the Naval Armory was designed by Georgia Tech architecture professors Harold Bush-Brown and Herbert C. Gailey, whose firm

ABOVE: *Naval Armory, Georgia Tech, Bush-Brown and Gailey, 1934-35 (CWA project) (photo courtesy of Navy ROTC, Georgia Tech)*

BELOW: *Folger Shakespeare Library, Washington, D.C., Paul P. Cret, 1932 (photo by Robert M. Craig)*

(later joined by Paul M. Heffernan) would play an active role in designing and building Georgia Tech campus structures from the 1930s through the mid-1950s.

The Naval Armory arranged offices in front of a 200-by-60-foot drill hall in a *T*-shaped layout oriented toward Third Street. Recognizing the impediments to practical naval training in an inland facility, the U.S. Navy set up in various areas of the armory "a model of a ship's bridge, a machine shop, a radio short wave station, a four inch destroyer type gun together with actual conditions of loading and firing by means of sub-caliber, a dismantled torpedo, a miniature whaleboat with davits, a periscope, and many other features which make for more thorough training of Tech men to be better and more efficient Reserve Officers through practical experience."[20]

Intended to be built by the unskilled workers of the CWA, the simple load-bearing brick walls were surfaced in concrete

principal facade, two relief panels depicted an airplane with bombs and a battleship, both of which survive, as archaeological relics of the CWA project, in a small garden enclave adjacent to the present Navy ROTC Building.

The new Georgia Tech Gymnasium and Auditorium, designed in 1934, was not immediately constructed due to an inability to develop funding until 1936.[21] Part of a larger $827,000 project announced in February 1936, 45 percent of which was to be financed by the PWA, the gymnasium was begun in June, and completed in February 1937 (see colorplate). It was the first reinforced-concrete structure on campus. A second phase of construction on the building was promised funding in September 1937, with Georgia Tech turning to both the WPA[22] and the PWA for assistance. Roosevelt finally authorized the grant in April 1938, with the second phase of the gymnasium completed in the following September. Georgia Tech added a swimming pool section in 1939.[23]

Matt Jorgenson of Bush-Brown and Gailey is credited with the executed design of the 1936-37 Georgia Tech Gymnasium and Auditorium, a design clearly derived from

ABOVE: *Bronze gates, Julian H. Harris, 1935 (from Naval Armory, Georgia Tech, now installed in Naval ROTC Building, old Ceramics Building, Georgia Tech) (photo by Robert M. Craig)*

AT RIGHT: *Gymnasium and Auditorium, Georgia Tech, Bush-Brown and Gailey, 1936-37 (PWA/WPA project) (photo from Robert M. Craig Collection, Atlanta History Center)*

parging in order to hide sloppy masonry. The material allowed the base to be given a striated rustication. The building was extremely plain, although sculptural enrichments accented the main facade. Above the Third Street entry was placed an eagle from the bow of the World War I battleship USS *Georgia*. Atlanta sculptor Julian H. Harris designed the bronze entry gates of the armory with metal from the same ship, and also provided relief panels to adorn the door enframement. The gates were reinstalled in the 1924 Ceramics Building, which today serves as the Navy ROTC Building on campus. Recessed in the center of the end bays of the original 1934-35 Naval Armory, above the second-floor windows of this

AT LEFT: *Relief panel, Julian H. Harris, 1935 (from Naval Armory, Georgia Tech, now in garden of Naval ROTC Building, old Ceramics Building, Georgia Tech) (photo by Robert M. Craig)*

BELOW: *Gymnasium and Auditorium, Georgia Tech, Matt Jorgenson rendering, Bush-Brown and Gailey, 1936-37 (PWA/WPA project) (courtesy of Georgia Tech Archives)*

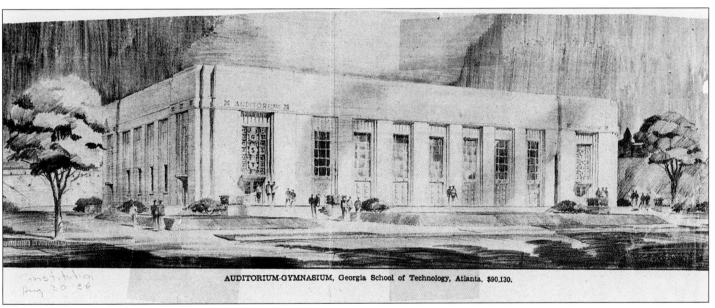

AUDITORIUM-GYMNASIUM, Georgia School of Technology, Atlanta, $90,130.

Paul Cret's Folger Shakespeare Library in Washington, D.C. The simple range of piers that extends across the main facade was flanked by doors at each end, accented by pierced grills of geometric outline with lettering of Deco-era precision. A noble attic capped the elevation, lending a monumentality to the massive block. Constructed of monolithic concrete resting on concrete piles, the whole remained economical in its elements and modern in its smooth surfaces. In fundamental ways, the design reflected the spirit of Cret's mediation between the classic and modern. Deeply rooted in the classical tradition, the Gymnasium and Auditorium translated a Hellenistic colonnaded stoa to contemporary use by way of Cret's Modern Classic Folger Library.

The Athletic Association Building (One Ninety Building), next door to the west, similarly reflected the reduced forms and tempered surfaces of the period. It was designed by Bush-Brown and Gailey, funded by the WPA, and completed in 1941.

Taking its cue from the earlier New Deal designs, the Athletic Association Building employed the striated rusticated base of the Naval Armory with the smooth concrete surfaces of both the armory and the gymnasium. Its door enframement, about the same size as that of the larger armory to the east, provided an ennobling focus for the entry, a simple and abstract portico of geometric definition. Completing a range of CWA/PWA/WPA projects, the building remained secondary to the centerpiece of the group, the Cret-inspired Gymnasium and Auditorium. Together these works composed a rare streetscape of New Deal-era Modern Classic edifices, simplified Modernistic structures that represented Georgia Tech's earliest gestures to architectural forms considered distinctly of the twentieth century.

Georgia Tech was able to complete additional buildings under PWA and WPA funding during the period, designed by architecture professors Bush-Brown and Gailey although in styles other than the Modern Classic: an addition to the Chemistry Building (1936, WPA, since razed), a Chemistry Laboratory (1939, PWA), and additions to the Ceramics Building (1939,

WPA), to Brittain Dining Hall (ODK Banquet Room) (1939-40, WPA), and to the Daniel Chemical Engineering Laboratory (1942, WPA). The most significant additional PWA project was a Modern design of Paul Heffernan, newly joining Bush-Brown and Gailey, for the Hinman Research Building, a work discussed in the following volume.[24]

Atlanta became the regional office of the PWA in the Southeast, one of seven centers created nationally to administer New Deal-financed projects. When Roosevelt was inaugurated president, his "first hundred days" legislation included the National Industrial Recovery Act, whose June 1933 Title II provided for Public Works and Construction Projects. Roosevelt's executive order #6174 created the Federal Emergency Administration of Public Works.

The intention of such programs, according to Harold Ickes (Secretary of Interior and head of the PWA), was "to put men to work, to do it quickly, and to do it intelligently."[25] When Roosevelt took the oath of office in March 1933, 15 million Americans were unemployed, including three-fourths of the building industry, whose construction activities had plummeted to less than 15 percent of the levels of five years earlier. The spiraling effect of this, according to Secretary Ickes, was that for each unemployed construction worker, another employee in a related industry was laid off, and a third level (in the auto industry, for example) was directly affected.[26] In Atlanta, new construction in 1933 was only 3 percent of the 1930 level of building activity.[27]

The problem was further exacerbated by the changing focus of the construction activity that was occurring. While about half of the building industry traditionally provided for residential use, by 1934 housing construction had dropped to 16 percent, despite increasing housing shortages, deteriorating and already substandard existing housing stock, and a rising population. Efforts to encourage private investment through the Emergency Relief and Reconstruction Act (1932) had proved insufficient, and it was not until the National Industrial Recovery Act (NIRA) of 1933 established a fund for direct subsidies for slum clearance and housing construction under the PWA that low- to middle-income workers found significant federal assistance to alleviate the housing crunch.

Atlanta's Techwood Homes for whites (1933-36) and University Homes for blacks (1934-36) were the first public housing projects approved by the PWA.[28] Completed in 1936, Techwood Homes is a work of national significance as the first federally funded slum clearance and public housing project in the United States.[29] Designed by Burge and Stevens in a modified Georgian style, the units sought to incorporate, with the greatest

Techwood Homes, Burge and Stevens, 1933-36 (photo from Robert M. Craig Collection, Atlanta History Center)

Techwood Homes, Burge and Stevens, 1933-36 (courtesy of Stevens & Wilkinson)

economy possible, the latest features of functionalist Modern design for housing. The units were two rooms deep in order to admit sunlight and fresh air, and occupied only about 20 percent of the available land, providing courtyards and landscaped open areas as more healthful alternatives to the crowded conditions of dense urban tenements. Their setback siting, flat roofs, reinforced-concrete-slab ceilings, steel window casings, and the easily cleaned and durable interior finishes and contemporary appliances all contributed to the project's modern character. Within a more traditional brick exterior of classic accent was a modern functional housing unit, a PWA Modern Classic project embodying the contemporary spirit of tradition modernized and the modern traditionalized.

In its government sponsorship and modern functional character, Techwood Homes echoed developments in European hous-

ing without fully incorporating its avant-garde aesthetic. Indeed, with its lack of ornament, simplified cubic forms, and flat roofs, contemporary University Homes by Edwards and Sayward presents simpler, perhaps more abstract if not aesthetically more progressive forms; it was certainly more restrained and economical. By contrast, Techwood Homes was criticized for its "unnecessary" use of limestone trim and other features thought to be excessive. Moreover, Burge and Stevens' first design for Techwood, dated September 1933, included a Techwood Dormitory for Georgia Tech, projected as a simplified Jacobean scheme of gabled brick residential units, much in the spirit of the nearby Brown (1925) and Harris (1926) dormitories by Bush-Brown and Gailey (or Burge and Stevens' own Chi Phi Fraternity House, 1928) at Georgia Tech. Further, the layout of this first scheme was nothing short of

BELOW: *Preliminary plan, Techwood Homes, Burge and Stevens, 1933-36 (courtesy of Stevens & Wilkinson)*

BOTTOM: *Revised plan, Techwood Homes, Burge and Stevens, 1933-36 (courtesy of Stevens & Wilkinson)*

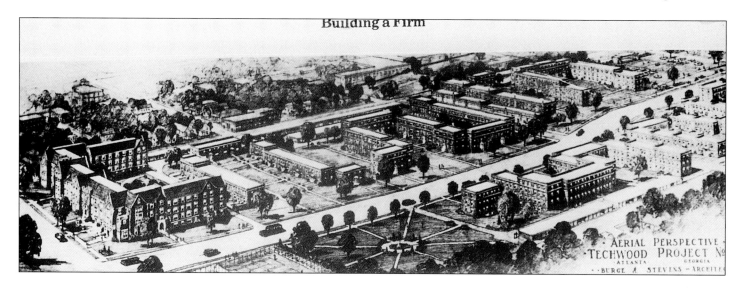

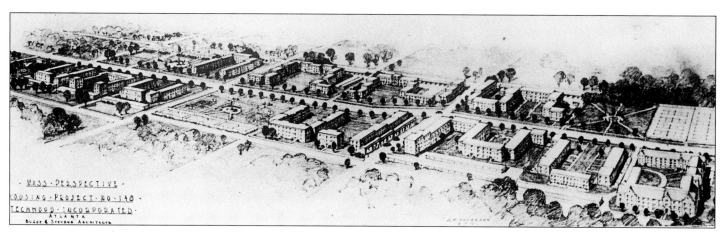

118

Beaux Arts, a formal configuration of geometric park areas, axes, and balanced units, albeit some buildings, in themselves, picturesquely composed.

When this more open plan of lower density and medieval forms was rejected by the government, Henry Wright, the noted planner and housing reformer serving as consultant to the Housing Division of the PWA, revised the scheme (April 17, 1934). He retained a number of amenities and much of Burge's building footprint, but added 108 apartments to one of Burge's parks and increased the project to 604 units organized throughout the plan in narrow, linear, setback blocks. The revised Techwood would be flat roofed; would be constructed in concrete and brick for fire safety; and would incorporate modern kitchens, indoor plumbing, and other features intended to improve the living conditions of its tenants. Surrounded by recreational areas and open lawns, Techwood reflected, as well, modern social ideals of providing outdoor areas to encourage interaction among tenants in a carefully planned environment.[30]

In addition, planners provided for an administration building with space for eight stores, including a grocery store, a bakery, a drugstore, a barber, and a hair salon for women, as well as medical and dental facilities. The basements of apartment units contained laundries, a library, meeting rooms, and storage. Children's fenced-in playgrounds, a wading pool, and a kindergarten were provided. For adults, a drama club, a community newspaper (*The Techwood News*), classes in adult education and physical fitness, and evening dances and songfests were also offered. "With these amenities," writes Techwood historian Carol Flores, and its "innovations in design and construction, Techwood Homes offered the most modern facilities in the city."[31]

Significantly, Techwood Homes served as a model, creating standards recommended by the government for fifty-eight other PWA projects nationally and voluntarily adopted by local housing administrators across the country.[32] But the federal government's chief focus and interest was in providing jobs, not providing affordable and progressive housing for low- and middle-income people. In fact, Charles Palmer, the Atlanta businessman turned housing reformer who initiated the Techwood project, commented in 1937 upon how minimal the federal government's involvement in providing affordable housing really was. Comparing twelve European countries with a total population equal to that of the United States, Palmer observed that between 1918 and 1937 the European governments had rehoused 20 million people while the United States PWA program had created a mere 22,000 units, or one-tenth of 1 percent of the European total.[33]

Nevertheless, in its efforts to provide jobs for the depressed construction industry, the PWA sponsored projects that extended considerably beyond housing. By the end of the decade, over 34,500 projects of various building types nationally would receive PWA support through grants and/or loans with an estimated benefit to the economy of seven billion dollars in new construction.[34] In addition to housing schemes, these included support for recreational buildings, post offices, courthouses, city halls, libraries, armories, memorials, and other local government buildings, as well as a series of engineering projects: dams, waterworks and sewage plants, highways and bridges, "and even shipbuilding, airplanes, and streamlined locomotives."[35]

Life Magazine noted that construction projects under the New Deal were so extensive that "Franklin D. Roosevelt has made Cheops, Pericles, Augustus, Chin Shih Huang Ti, the Medicis, and Peter the Great look like a club of birdhouse-builders." The *Life* reporter went on to imply that the PWA had bettered the achievements of the ancient great builders: for every Great Pyramid, Great Wall of China, or Parthenon, the PWA produced enormous hydroelectric dams, "glistening" civic structures from courthouses to post offices, numerous schools, city halls, and an American highway system that significantly surpassed the accomplishments of ancient Roman engineers.[36]

The PWA and the WPA are often confused, most certainly because of the juxtaposition of letters in their abbreviations. As previously noted,[37] historians have referenced the latter in ascribing a "WPA Classic" style to New Deal architecture, under the assumption that the WPA either supported or aesthetically influenced buildings in question. While there is definitely a depression-era modern/classic aesthetic that differs from populist Art Deco (see chapter 2), as well as from both the industrial-design-inspired Streamlined Moderne and the Bauhaus-inspired radical Modern (see the following volume), the Modern Classic is not restricted to New Deal public works. The WPA competed with the PWA for funds, but the WPA's architectural impact was less than that of the PWA. Moreover, the two agencies overlapped in purpose: the WPA directly hired architects to design buildings and funded their construction, but most of the federally funded projects assumed to be WPA were in fact PWA-financed.

Furthermore, the murals and sculpture adorning federal buildings of the era were neither WPA nor PWA but were executed under the direction of the Treasury Department's Section of Painting and Sculpture, later known as the Section of Fine Arts.[38] Established in 1934 and in existence until 1943, the Section commissioned art for 1,100 post offices nationally, particularly those in small cities and towns. State and municipal buildings in larger cities were more likely to be adorned by WPA-sponsored art under the Federal Art Project.

Similar to such art throughout the country, art in Georgia's post offices displayed three types of subjects: contemporary workers (especially farm scenes and farm laborers in agricultural states such as Georgia), panoramas of town and countryside, and scenes reflecting local history. Artists were selected usually by competition from sketches and encouraged to negotiate themes with local citizens. New Deal art in the Atlanta area includes a 1938 mural by Jack McMillen (b. 1910) in the post office in College Park entitled *Arrival of Atlanta and West Point Railroad*; a 1940 mural, now in the old railroad depot at Conyers, painted by Elizabeth Terrell (b. 1908) entitled *The Ploughman*; and two murals moved to the Richard Russell Building in Atlanta, *Dogwood and Azalea* (1938), originally painted by Paul Rohland (1884-1953) for the Decatur Post Office, and *Spring in Georgia* (1942), painted by Andree Ruellan (b. 1905) for the Lawrenceville Post Office.[39] The Treasury Department's Section of Painting and Sculpture sponsored such works because it was this federal department that was responsible for the construction and decoration of federal buildings.

Treasury architects might employ a "federal modern classic style," but records of New Deal-financed buildings in general do not show an adequate conformity to common formal or decorative elements to justify suggestions that there emerged an official PWA style. Projects in Colonial Revival, Georgian Revival, and Spanish Colonial Revival were built in numerous locales. But a spirit of economy of detail and planning functionalism influenced a restrained character in typical works of the period. A 1939 survey of PWA projects noted that "the outstanding accomplishments in planning of both Federal and non-Federal buildings are the elimination of waste space, economy in cost, and proper consideration of light, ventilation, and sanitation; while in design, careful study of line, scale, and proportion, greater simplicity and extremely sparing use of ornament, and a skillful and effective handling of materials, are noteworthy characteristics."[40] Excessive ornamentation was seen to be unnecessary and a detraction from the aesthetic values of a building.

Schools especially benefited from federal financing, such that "by 1936 over seventy percent of all school construction in the U.S. came through the PWA."[41] In Atlanta three

new schools were constructed through the New Deal with more than a dozen others benefiting from New Deal programs, which supported various classroom (and other) additions made to established schools. New cafeterias, gymnasiums, and auditoriums, as well as science laboratories, art studios, or music rooms to support expanded curricula, reflected progressive ideas concerning a "modern education."[42]

E. L. Connally Elementary School (1936-37), designed by Jesse Wilhoit in simplified medieval forms of an English vernacular style, was the first new Atlanta school built under the WPA. Its simple gabled forms echoed nearby Gothic Revival church design, and its projecting elements and informal plan provided a picturesque domesticity, bringing the character and scale of the school into harmony with its residential neighborhood. Stone trim was employed to enframe the entry porch and to cap end gables and a wall dormer. The roof was slate, and several windows were positioned under neo-Gothic pointed arches with quatrefoils set in the tympana. The architect enlivened wall surfaces with herringbone and basket-weave brick patterns; in general, a variegated brickwork, with blackened glazed surfaces or warm orange tones, ensured a craftsmanly aesthetic that was simple and appealing. The additions of auditorium/gymnasium/cafeteria and classrooms in 1947-48 by Wilhoit

TOP: *E. L. Connally Elementary School, Jesse Wilhoit, 1936-37 (WPA project) (photo from Robert M. Craig Collection, Atlanta History Center)*

and Smith were sensitive in scale and material finish.

Wilhoit's medieval vernacular helps underscore the stylistic variety of New Deal architecture, and the inability to apply a term such as "WPA Classic" or "PWA Classic" to period works built under these federal agencies. But there is an economy of line in thirties design that in part is governed by efforts to avoid extravagance and in part reflects an increasingly simple modern trend in architectural forms.

Two 1938 schools reflected these tendencies within classical vocabularies, the Garden Hills Elementary School, a WPA project designed by Tucker and Howell, and the Haygood Elementary School (now Atlanta Union Mission for Women), built under the WPA program to designs by Ivey and Crook. Garden Hills sought to fit comfortably in a neighborhood of Colonial Revival, Georgian Revival, and neoclassical residences. It represents a traditional work by a firm that, following World War II, would turn enthusiastically to Modern design with its Morris Brandon (1946-47) and Emma Hutchinson (1955-56) elementary schools.

At Ivey and Crook's 1938 Haygood

School, a geometric entry block presented abstract forms as restrained as John Soane's early-nineteenth-century minimalist neoclassicism at Dulwich, but Haygood maintained a distinctly Modernistic air. Its projections are barely defined by shadows whose lines mark setbacks and fluted zigzag recesses flanking the door. A telescopic needle, itself a setback profile, capped the pyramid roof of the entry block. A delicate abstract floral band and almost unnoticed piecrust trim provided a faint echo of Deco relief patterns. Flanking wings projected only the air of a factory for education. But by the time H. Griffith Edwards added the 1949-50 Auditorium at the north end of the building, the fourth progressive modern style, European-inspired Modernism, was entering into the consciousness of Atlanta architects and being manifested in built works. The Edwards design adds a dynamism to the streetscape and corner and is highly successful.

Some depression-era Modern Classic forms continued to mark school entries, shape light fixtures, and accent walls with setback profiles or restrained classic piers as late as the late 1940s. The modernization of an older school, such as the Ed S. Cook

Garden Hills Elementary School, Tucker and Howell, 1938 (WPA project) (photo by Robert M. Craig)

Haygood Elementary School, Ivey and Crook, 1938 (WPA project) (photo by Robert M. Craig)

BELOW: *Rendering for remodeling, Ed S. Cook Elementary School, Ivey and Crook, 1945 (courtesy of the Atlanta History Center)*

BOTTOM: *Ed S. Cook Elementary School (1911), remodeling by Ivey and Crook, 1945-48 (photo from Robert M. Craig Collection, Atlanta History Center)*

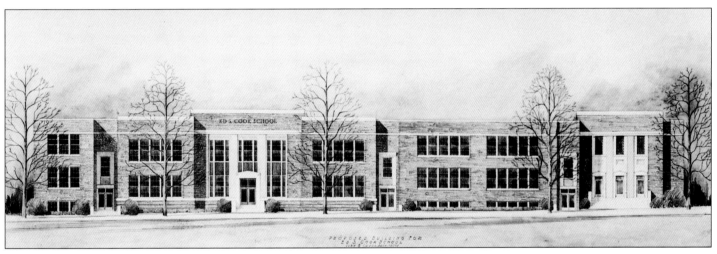

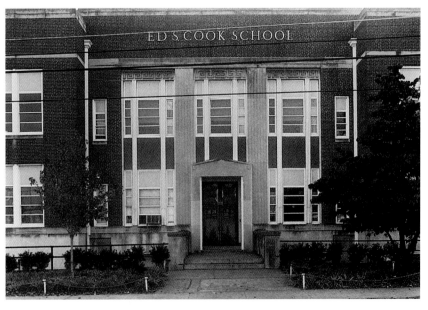

Elementary School of 1911, resulted in a transitional and hybrid composition. Commissioned in 1945 and executed by Ivey and Crook in 1947-48, the alterations remained conservative, the work of traditional architects not ready to employ the forms of the new postwar Modernists. At Ed S. Cook School's remodeling, Ivey and Crook remained Modern Classic, redressing an established school in Greek frets and pilasters, a fashion already growing old in the view of a younger generation of architects.

By the late 1940s, Modern forces were beginning to modulate the established aesthetic, and hybrid designs accompanied the

J. C. Murphy High School, Barili and Humphreys, 1947-49 (porte cochere, Jova/Daniels/Busby, 1987) (photo from Robert M. Craig Collection, Atlanta History Center)

Greybar Electric Building, Gilbert Beers, builder, 1949 (photo from Robert M. Craig Collection, Atlanta History Center)

arrival of a postwar Modernism. J. C. Murphy High School of 1947-49 (best known for its providing the setting in the 1960s for Atlanta's first public school integration) was built in a style that only begins to anticipate the Modern in the continuity of its composed bands of windows. But despite its string-courses, pilasters, and trim accents recalling the Modern Classic, Murphy High School was also punctuated with vertical entry forms of setback profile, which were more Deco than Modern Classic. Murphy, built in the closing years of the 1940s, remained a hybrid composition of conservative forms of the 1930s. It offers an interesting parallel to a comparable design at the Greybar Electric Building (1949).

At Greybar, extended horizontal bands appear to slide behind the Deco setback entry bays and bring a dynamic continuity to the building. Murphy High School's windows are grouped but remain vertical in their individual proportions, and are thus legible as bays rather than volumetric screens or parts of a continuous horizontal flow. Greybar, on the other hand, relates its dynamic lines to the roadside, in the spirit of the Moderne, but without Moderne's streamlined forms and rounded corners. The cantilevered semicircular canopy at Greybar (the canopy at Murphy is ca. 1989) is its only curved line, but the building remains less static than the Modern Classic and speaks to the flow of traffic.

The late employment of the Modern Classic aesthetic reflected a formal tie to the past in the face of a mid-1940s interest in the most avant-garde modern styles. This was the stark, volumetric, ahistoric, and functionalist style of Modernism. The Modern Classic remained a more conservative effort to modernize the traditional and traditionalize the modern; in spirit, it retains a thirties character.

For example, Atlanta's red brick Municipal Auditorium (1907-9), which had been completely renovated with WPA assistance in 1938, was altered for use by Georgia State University and given a new facade in 1943 designed by Robert and Co. (see colorplate). In its newest dress, the auditorium (now Alumni Hall) displayed a smooth cladding of clean white surfaces organized with classic balance. The stepped forms of the building's entry front climb the hill in regulated gaits. The extended horizontal lines of the foundation stretch unbroken the length of the block, further unifying the broken masses above.

The abstinence from ornament and color at Alumni Hall reflects a modern austerity and abstraction but without the language of Bauhaus ribbon windows, continuous sun screens, and machine imagery by which nearby Sparks Hall of 1952-55 declares itself a child of International Style Modernism. By the mid-1950s, the Modern style had established itself in Atlanta, especially

Alumni Hall, Georgia State University (formerly Municipal Auditorium), new facade, Robert and Co., 1943 (photo from Robert M. Craig Collection, Atlanta History Center)

125

Sparks Hall, Georgia State University, Cooper, Bond, and Cooper, 1952-55 (originally two stories) (photo from Robert M. Craig Collection, Atlanta History Center)

State Highway Board Building, A. Ten Eyck Brown, 1931 (photo by Robert M. Craig)

in school architecture, and only the most conservative sponsors retained the "traditional modern" for public and institutional architecture.

The same slow shift from Modern Classic to Modern, suggested by Georgia State University's Alumni Hall and Sparks Hall, is evidenced in the several state office buildings

built on sites flanking the Georgia State Capitol, with the Transportation Building ultimately adopting the most progressive forms in the group. The earliest building of the group is the State Highway Board Building of 1931, designed by A. Ten Eyck Brown and located at #2 Capitol Square, southeast of the State Capitol. A reinforced-concrete structure, its original entry faced northeast at the clipped corner of the building and established in its marble cladding the white facing material of classically restrained government buildings soon to fill flanking city blocks.

Augustus E. Constantine followed Brown's Modern Classic precedent in his 1939 design for the Administration Building of the Federal Emergency Administration of

127

Public Works, erected just west of the State Highway Board Building. This 1939 F.E.R.A. Building is distinguished by six panels of figures against black marble executed by noted Atlanta sculptor Julian H. Harris. Formal architectural elements remained sparing on the state office buildings built in 1954 on nearby sites by A. Thomas Bradbury (R. E. Slay, associate): the Law and Justice Building (southwest of the Capitol and including the 244 and 254 Washington Street buildings) and the Agriculture Building (on the east side). Again, Julian H. Harris provided remarkable figural sculpture flanking the entry of the Agriculture Building, panels nicknamed "Adam" and "Eve" by the sculptor's young children, but which represent Animal Husbandry and Agriculture (Farming). The classical door enframements and Modernistic neo-grec sculpture connect these buildings to a humanist tradition, and a minimalist monumentality is achieved by the rhythm of piers and windows.

In 1958 A. Thomas Bradbury added to the

complex the Health Building (47 Trinity Ave., see photo, page 80), and Bradbury and Associates completed their work with the Trinity-Washington Building in 1965-66. The prevailing spirit of these state office buildings was increasingly abstract, a faceless bureaucracy of officialdom deriving its architectural dress from a reduction of building form to colorless wall plane. By the time Bradbury designed the Georgia Department of History and Archives Building in 1962-65, the result of this modernization of classicism, this process of elimination, was a box, an elemental form but a boring one as well. In the end these modernized traditional surfaces were becoming less satisfying designs than the overlapping planar constructions of contemporary and committed Modernists who at least conveyed in their work a sense of being progressive.

Among the state office buildings it was only the Department of Transportation Headquarters that reflected the machine aesthetic of Modernism, an architectural embodiment, perhaps, of the engineering activity within. The State Highway Department was alone willing to introduce the machine to the classical environment of the state complex, and did so as early as 1947 when A. Ten Eyck Brown's 1931 building was extended northward along the east side of Capitol Place. The slab eyelid sun screens behind Brown's building are features of the Modern, not the Modern Classic, and offer cues to A. Thomas Bradbury's later additions to the Transportation complex.

Bradbury's 1957 Transportation Building, with its offices and parking garage hidden behind Modern ribbon windows, wraps Bauhaus-inspired surfaces along Capitol

State Agriculture Building (A. Thomas Bradbury, architect; R. E. Slay, associate architect; sculpture by Julian H. Harris), 1954 (photo by Robert M. Craig)

129

Georgia Department of History and Archives Building, A. Thomas Bradbury, 1962-65 (photo by Robert M. Craig)

130

Avenue and presents an image that crosses stylistically beyond the rationalist purity of neoclassicism toward a Modern "International Style" abstraction. The principal forms of the southeast face of the Transportation Building sweep with deliberate rationalist detachment around the corner of the block, causing the structure to turn its back on its neoclassical neighbors. It is a different modernism.

The administrative headquarters of the highway department faces southeast, overlooking not the humanist marble forms of the Capitol but the concrete slabs and bridge abutments of the expressway. From within the Transportation Building, there are no views of the great governmental dome nor of trees and statues in surrounding Capitol grounds. Rather, the engineers look from Modern strip windows at distant miles of unbroken interstate highway. Even that view has lately been marred by the insensitive addition of an obtrusive pedestrian bridge of Late-Modern steel frame. Those who have suffered state transportation intrusions into traditional neighborhoods would find these various features of the Transportation Department's Capitol grounds construction highly symbolic.

The bureaucratic architectural forms of A. Thomas Bradbury's Modern Classic state office buildings present white walls of such austerity that their monumentality is constantly at odds with a sense of passionless modern abstraction. In a similar way, the absolute simplicity of the 1959-60 Masonic Temple marks a composition of archaic, fundamental forms that falls short of an intended monumentality, although its neoclassical detail offers conciliatory reward. Designed by Cooper, Barrett, Skinner, Woodbury, and Cooper, Inc., the Masonic Temple reflects the Masonic Order's traditional roots in ancient classicism, its symbolism, its rites, and its humanism. But the Temple is treated with such control and moderation, and it is detailed with such minimalism, that a resulting abstraction promotes a reading in its forms of modern influences as well. It joins the state office buildings at Capitol Square in positioning the late Modern Classic at the

State Highway Board Building Extension, 1947 (photo by Robert M. Craig)

edge of the more bland and uninspired Modern of the late 1950s and 1960s. What would follow the Deco-to-Modern era was a second generation of Bauhaus-trained practitioners, or at least students of the Bauhaus generation. This new wave of architects was a group of designers whose education was based more on values of standardization and mass production, and whose aesthetic sensitivities and abilities were less well grounded in history and craftsmanship. Ornament, whether neoclassical or Deco appliqué, was to be displaced by an abstract beauty of economic line, usable space, and nontraditional artistic minimalism.

The functionalist early Modern style, to which this younger generation subscribed, was born in 1920s Germany and, as Tom

131

ABOVE: *Transportation Building, A. Thomas Bradbury, 1956-57 (photo by Robert M. Craig)*

AT RIGHT: *Masonic Temple, Cooper, Barrett, Woodbury, Skinner, and Cooper, Inc., 1959-60 (photo by Robert M. Craig)*

Wolfe has observed, emigrated "from Bauhaus to our house."[43] It represented one of two mechanistic phases of progressive architecture during the "Deco to Modern" period, both of which moved beyond traditional-bound Art Deco and Modern Classic. The first machine-modern style, appearing in Atlanta in the late 1930s, was the roadside architecture of the Streamlined Moderne inspired by developments in industrial design. The second, emerging in Atlanta in the late 1940s (after the end of World War II offered a new beginning), was the revolutionary functionalist aesthetic of the International Style, or simply Modern.

Significant differences in design inspiration and aesthetic intention distinguish the Moderne from the Modern, just as both vary in significant ways from Art Deco and Modern Classic. Art Deco and Modern Classic may be viewed more conservatively, as progressive reflections of traditional interpretations which viewed architecture as "ornamented construction." On the other hand, both the Streamlined Moderne and the Modern looked to modern machinery to inspire an efficiency of form, a technological expression, and a functional design viewed as ideally suited to the twentieth century. Whatever cosmetic effects were employed to achieve the new streamlining, the aesthetic intention of artists was to create dynamic forms—a functional expression that fused ornament to form, rather than applying artistic decoration to formal surfaces. The new progressive designers of the third phase of modernism found inspiration in modern science and technology, industrial and transportation forms, and a new spirit of American mobility. Above all, Streamlined Moderne was the style of the automobile.

An even more abstract functionalism and machine aesthetic characterized the fourth progressive style, the Modern, separating it even further from the comparatively more conservative Art Deco and Modern Classic. If Deco and Modern Classic kept one eye on the past, Streamlined Moderne and Modern sought especially to express a contemporary, modern, even futuristic aesthetic; the Modern recognized itself as revolutionary. Advances in science and technology encouraged new hopes in a new age, and a new promise for the "world of tomorrow." As the premier city of the New South, recovering from the Great Depression and beginning a new life after World War II, Atlanta would embrace the Streamlined Moderne and then the Modern style as architectural manifestations of a reinvigorated progressivism.

Classical strains persisted. In a conservative city of traditional values, citizens continued to prefer conventional, frequently classical, styles for their homes, and the use of the conservative Modern Classic for governmental projects carried on throughout the 1950s in the state office buildings near the Capitol. However, with increasingly fervent ambitions to move Atlanta forward, a new generation of progressive designers and clients left Art Deco and Modern Classic behind after the war. Beginning to shape Atlanta's urban forms in a new Modernism, a new wave of architects prepared the way for the city to establish a position of aesthetic leadership in the region. The new Atlanta images were technological ones—mechanistic, abstract, and progressive. The new age of Atlanta's architecture evolved from Moderne to Modern.

Appendix

The information below is taken from the 1931, 1936, 1941, 1947, 1951, and 1956 City Directories, which list architects as surveyed during the fall of the previous year. (There was no 1946 City Directory.)

ARCHITECTS IN ATLANTA, 1930
*will not still be listed by 1935; [*] later reappears

Richard W. Alger* (Marye, Alger, and Vinour)
Haralson Bleckley*
George Harwell Bond
A. Ten Eyck Brown
Burge and Stevens
William J. J. Chase
Edouard Clerk*
Cooper and Cooper
Park A. Dallas and Co.*
Daniell and Beutell
Edwards and Sayward
Alexander F. N. Everett
Frazier and Bodin
Hentz, Adler and Shutze
John Hill*
Lodowick J. Hill, Jr.
Charles H. Hopson
Ivey and Crook
Arthur J. Jones*
Henry H. Jordon
Ernest W. King*
Lockwood* and Poundstone
R. B. Logan[*]
Marye, Vinour, Marye, and Armistead*
McDonald and Co.*
James T. Mitchell*
R. S. Monday*
Morgan,* Dillon, and Lewis
Isaac Moscowitz[*]
Fred J. Orr*
William C. Pauley (landscape)*

R. Kennon Perry
G. Lloyd Preacher and Co, Inc.*
Pringle* and Smith
Robert and Co., Inc.
Arthur Neal Robinson
James M. Russell*
Arthur W. Smith
Cyril B. Smith
DeFord Smith*
Silas D. Trowbridge*
Tucker and Howell
Eugene C. Wachendorff[*]
Leila R. Wilburn
Jesse Wilhoit

ARCHITECTS IN ATLANTA, 1935
**not previously listed in 1930; *will not still be listed by 1940

Alfredo Barili, Jr.**
George Harwell Bond
A. Thomas Bradbury**
A. Ten Eyck Brown*
Burge and Stevens
William J. J. Chase
Augustus E. Constantine**/*
John A. Cooksey**/*
Cooper and Cooper
Daniell and Beutell
John R. Dillon and Edward S. Lewis
Edwards* and Sayward
Alexander F. N. Everett*
Frazier and Bodin
Will W. Griffin**/*
Hentz, Adler and Shutze
Lodowick J. Hill, Jr.
Charles H. Hopson
J. Wharton Humphreys**
Ivey and Crook
Henry G. Jacobs**/*

Henry H. Jordon
P. Thornton Marye*
R. Kennon Perry
Odis Poundstone
Robert and Co., Inc.
Arthur Neal Robinson
Emil C. Seiz**/*
Arthur W. Smith*
Cyril B. Smith
Francis P. Smith
Norman F. Stambaugh**
Tucker and Howell
Arthur F. Walker**/*
Leila R. Wilburn
Jesse Wilhoit
James C. Wise**
Linton H. Young**

ARCHITECTS IN ATLANTA, 1940

**not previously listed in 1935; *will not still be listed by 1946; [*] not in architects section in 1946, but known to continue in practice

Richard L. Aeck**
Barili and Humphreys
George Harwell Bond
A. Thomas Bradbury[*]
Burge and Stevens
Thomas M. Campbell**/*
William J. J. Chase
Cooper and Cooper
David S. Cuttino, Jr.**
John C. Daniel (Decatur)**/*
Daniell and Beutell*
John R. Dillon and Edward S. Lewis*
Edwards and Goodwyne**/*
Theo B. Fay**/*
Walter L. Felch**/*
Clement J. Ford**/[*]
J. Claud Foster**/*
William M. Frazier**
Frazier* and Bodin
Hentz, Adler and Shutze* (Shutze and
    Armistead 1945-50)
Lodowick J. Hill, Jr.*
Charles H. Hopson*
Ivey and Crook
Henry H. Jordon
Willard N. Lamberson**
Harold C. McLaughlin**/*
Isaac Moscowitz**

R. Kennon Perry
Odis Poundstone
Warren C. Powell**/*
Robert and Co., Inc.
Arthur N. Robinson (Sr. and Jr.**)
Sayward and Logan**
William Walter Simmons**
Cyril B. Smith*
Francis P. Smith
Smith* and Daves**
Smith and Sorrells Inc.**/*
Norman F. Stambaugh
Henry J. Toombs**
Tucker and Howell
Eugene C. Wachendorff**
Leila R. Wilburn
Jesse Wilhoit
James C. Wise
Albert P. Woodard**/[*]
Linton H. Young

ARCHITECTS IN ATLANTA, 1946

**not previously listed in 1940; [**] one partner not listed in 1940; *will not still be listed by 1950; [*] not in architects section in 1950, but known to continue in practice

Abreu and Robinson**
Richard L. Aeck
Barili and Humphreys
George G. Blau, Jr.**
Bodin and Lamberson
Burge and Stevens [Stevens and Wilkinson
    after 1947]
Bush-Brown, Gailey, and Heffernan**
William J. J. Chase
John W. Cherry**
Cooper, Bond, and Cooper
Cuttino, Howard[**], and Ellis[**]
Francis M. Daves and Associates
H. Griffith Edwards
William M. Frazier*
Wilfred J. Gregson**
John J. Harte Co.**
Ivey and Crook
Jes R. Johnston, Jr.**/*
Henry H. Jordon
Wilfred L. Keel**
C. Hines MacArthur**/*
McDonald and Co.**
R. E. Moore and Co.**/*

Moscowitz and Wilner[**]
Percy H. Perkins, Jr.**/[*]
R. Kennon Perry
Poundstone, Ayers[**], and Godwin[**]
G. Lloyd Preacher and Associates**
Robert and Co., Inc.
Arthur N. Robinson (Sr. and Jr.)
Sayward, Logan, and Williams[**]/*
Shutze & Armistead [Philip Trammell
    Shutze after 1950]
William Walter Simmons
Arthur W. Smith**/*
Clarence A. Smith**/*
Francis P. Smith
Smith and Hobbs**
Norman F. Stambaugh
Toombs and Creighton[**]
Tucker and Howell
Eugene C. Wachendorff[*]
Leila R. Wilburn
Jesse Wilhoit
Wilhoit and Smith[**]
James C. Wise
Young and Fuller[**/*]

ARCHITECTS IN ATLANTA, 1950

**not previously listed in 1946; [**] one partner not
listed in 1946; *will not still be listed by 1955; [*] not
in architects section in 1955, but known to continue
in practice

Abreu and Robinson
Aeck Associates Architects
Alexander and Rothschild**
Armistead and Saggus[**]
Barili and Humphreys
Willie R. Biggers**/*
George G. Blau, Jr.
Bodin and Lamberson
A. Thomas Bradbury**
Builders Service Co.**/*
Bush-Brown, Gailey, and Heffernan*
Frank C. Bussey**/*
William J. J. Chase
John W. Cherry
Paul Q. Coker**/*
Cooper, Bond[*], and Cooper
William J. Creighton**/*
David S. Cuttino, Jr., and Associates
Vincent A. Daley**
Francis M. Daves and Associates

H. Griffith Edwards
W. L. Felch**/* [returns to practice]
Finch and Barnes**
Clement J. Ford** [returns to practice]
Fuller and Beckett**
Jas A. Giglio**/*
Lawton Grant Associates**/*
Charles M. Graves**/*
Hal Wyche Greer**
Gregson and Ellis[*]
John M. Harley**
John J. Harte Co.*
William C. Hay**/*
Ross H. Howard
Flynn E. Hudson**/*
Ivey and Crook
Henry H. Jordon
Wilfred L. Keel
W. G. Knoebel**/*
William F. Letson**/*
Locatell, Summer, and Co.**
Logan and Williams**
Lyles, Bissett, Carlisle and Wolff A&E &
    Robert French Assoc.**/*
McDonald and Co.
James Means**/[*]
Edward C. Miller**
Miller and Miller**
Moscowitz[*], Wilner, and Millkey[**]
S. Walton Peabody (Decatur)**/*
R. Kennon Perry*
Pollard and Altobellis**/*
Poundstone, Ayers, and Godwin*
G. Lloyd Preacher and Associates
G. Lloyd Preacher, Jr., and Co.**
Frank C. Puckett**/*
Robert and Co., Associates**
Robert and Co., Inc.*
Arthur N. Robinson (Sr. and Jr.)
B. E. Robuck, Inc.**/*
Ernest N. Rogers**/*
Charles W. Russ**/*
Philip Trammell Shutze
W. W. Simmons and Associates**/*
R. E. Slay**
Small Homes Plan Service**/*
Cyril B. Smith**/*
Francis P. Smith
Moreland Smith**
Smith and Hobbs, Inc. A&E*

Southern Engineering Co.**/*
Deryk P. Spiker**/*
Norman F. Stambaugh
Stevens and Wilkinson[**]
Toombs and Co.
Tucker and Howell
John W. Vaught**
June W. Wicker**
Leila R. Wilburn
Wilhoit and Smith
Isaac W. Wilkinson**
Wilkinson-Penny and Taylor**/*
James C. Wise
Linton H. Young

ARCHITECTS IN ATLANTA, 1955

**not previously listed in 1950; [**] one partner not
listed in 1950 or returned to practice

Abreu and Robinson
Aeck Associates
Alexander and Rothschild
Armistead and Saggus
Sanford M. Ayers**
Ayers and Godwin
Bank Design Inc.**
Barili and Humphreys
Barker and Cunningham**
Miller D. Barnes**
William S. Beckett**
Blau and Hall[**]
Bodin and Lamberson
A. Thomas Bradbury
William J. J. Chase
John W. Cherry
John A. Cooksey[**]
Cooper, Barrett, Skinner, Woodbury, and
    Cooper, Inc.**
Charles W. Cunningham**
John H. Cunningham**
Cuttino and Associates—Architects
Vincent A. Daley
Francis M. Daves and Associates
J. Frederick Dugger III**
H. Griffith Edwards
Finch and Barnes
Clement J. Ford
Pope H. Fuller**
Fuller and Beckett
Thomas E. Garner**
Robert W. Gibeling**

Clarence H. Glass**
James B. Godwin
Hal Wyche Greer
Wilfred I. Gregson**
Gregson and Associates
Griffin and Kjorling**
John M. Harley
Heery and Heery**
Ross H. Howard
Samuel T. Hurst**
Chester E. Hutchins, Jr.**
Ivey and Crook
N. A. Jacobs, Jr.**
Charles W. Jenkins**
Edward Johns**
Henry H. Jordon
Wilfred L. Keel
Thomas G. Little**
Locatell Inc.
Logan and Williams
Ernest O. Mastin**
Mastin and Summer**
Marion L. Matthews*
McDonald and Co.
A. Preston McIntosh**
Edward C. Miller
Miller and Miller
Henry D. Norris**
Warren F. Penney**
Percy H. Perkins, Jr.[**]
Robert B. Plunkett**
John C. Portman, Jr.**
G. Lloyd Preacher and Associates
G. Lloyd Preacher, Jr., and Co.
Herbert A. Rawlins**
Robert and Co., Associates
Arthur N. Robinson (Sr. and Jr.)
H. C. Rosenberg Associates**
David O. Savini**
Philip Trammell Shutze
R. E. Slay
Francis P. Smith
Moreland Smith
Richard J. Snelling**
Zenas A. Snipes, Jr.**
Herman H. Sorrells**
Stambaugh and Jett[**]
Stevens and Wilkinson
John R. Street**
John E. Summer**

John H. Summer**
Romulus H. Thompson**
Toombs, Amisano** and Wells**
Tucker and Howell
John W. Vaught
Eugene C. Wachendorff[**]
Jos Walker Co.**
Wells and Taylor**

June W. Wicker
Leila R. Wilburn
Wilhoit and Smith
Isaac W. Wilkinson
Wilner and Millkey
Philip B. Windsor**
James C. Wise
Linton H. Young

Notes

CHAPTER 1

1. Franklin M. Garrett, *Atlanta and Environs: A Chronicle of Its People and Events*, 3 vols. (New York: Lewis Historical Publishing Company, Inc., 1954). *See also* Dana F. White and Timothy J. Crimmins, eds., special issue on Atlanta urban history of *The Atlanta Historical Journal* 26, no. 2-3 (Summer-Fall 1982).

2. Barbara Baer Capitman, *Deco Delights: The Beauty and Joy of Miami Beach Architecture* (New York: E. P. Dutton, 1988).

3. Laura Cerwinske, *Tropical Deco: The Architecture and Design of Old Miami Beach* (New York: Rizzoli, 1981).

4. Atlanta's Chamber of Commerce monthly magazine, *The City Builder*, in June 1930 reported 2,115,848 building permits issued in Atlanta, 847,063 in New Orleans, 381,910 in Birmingham, and 168,400 in Miami; nine of the eighteen cities were west of the Mississippi River in Texas, Oklahoma, Missouri, and Kansas and eight of these held positions two through nine on the list. Atlanta's population of 359,668 was only surpassed by New Orleans (451,634) in 1930 among eight top Southeastern cities, including Louisville (307,808), Houston (289,428), Dallas (260,397), Birmingham (257,657), San Antonio (254,561), and Memphis (252,049).

5. John Ruskin, *The Seven Lamps of Architecture* (New York: Farrar, Straus and Cudahy, 1961 [first published 1849]), 16.

6. The Jefferson County Courthouse in Birmingham, Alabama, for example, dates from 1929-32 and is already evidencing stylistic characteristics of the Modern Classic. It is the work of the Chicago firm of Holabird and Root (with Jack B. Smith, associated architect), and displays remarkable Modernistic bas-relief panels by Chicago sculptor Les Friedlander. On the other side of Capitol Park stands Charles McCauley's late (1950) Modern Classic Birmingham City Hall.

7. Martin Greif, *Depression Modern: The Thirties Style in America* (New York: Universe Books, 1975).

8. Donald J. Bush, *The Streamlined Decade: Design in the Nineteen Thirties* (New York: George Braziller, 1975).

9. Richard Wurts, *The New York World's Fair 1939-1940 in 155 Photographs* (New York: Dover Publications, Inc., 1977).

10. Robert M. Craig, "Transportation Imagery and Streamlined Moderne Architecture: A Case for a Design Typology," in *Roadside America: The Automobile in Design and Culture*, ed. Jan Jennings (Ames, Iowa: Iowa State University Press, 1992), 15-28.

11. Henry-Russell Hitchcock and Philip Johnson, *The International Style* (New York: W. W. Norton, 1932); Walter Gropius, *The New Architecture and the Bauhaus* (Cambridge, Mass.: MIT Press, 1965) (first published London: Faber and Faber, 1935); and Tom Wolfe, *From Bauhaus to Our House* (New York: Farrar, Straus and Giroux, 1981). The Bauhaus was founded by Walter Gropius in April 1919 in Weimar, Germany. For more information about the Bauhaus, see chapter four, note 43 below.

CHAPTER 2

Chapter opening quotes are from: Forrest F.

Lisle, Jr., "Chicago's 'Century of Progress' Exposition: The Moderne as Democratic Popular Culture" (abstract of a paper presented at the Twenty-fifth Annual Meeting of the Society of Architectural Historians, San Francisco, January 26-30, 1972), *Journal of the Society of Architectural Historians* 31, no. 3 (October 1972): 230; Harold R. Shurtleff, quoted in *The Skyscraper Style*, Rosemarie Haag Bletter and Cervin Robinson (New York: Oxford University Press, 1975), 16; Alfred H. Barr, quoted in *Modern Architecture—International Exhibition*, Henry-Russell Hitchcock, Jr., et al. (Salem, N.H.: Ayer, 1970), 13 (quoted Bletter, 43).

1. Among the nation's noteworthy Art Deco people's palaces, the masterworks of popular modernism, were (and remain today) Los Angeles's Bullocks-Wiltshire Department Store (1928), St. Louis's Park Plaza Hotel (1929), New York City's Waldorf Astoria Hotel (1930), and Oakland, California's Paramount Theater (1930). Each provided its city at the end of the 1920s with a landmark of an emerging modernism, a modern ornamental style that in its expressive glitz and sensual colorism endeared it to a citizenry receptive to gleam, glitter, and stylishness.

2. Ruskin, *The Seven Lamps*, 16.

3. The first of several expansions for the high school was sponsored by the WPA and designed by Wachendorff in 1937, adding six classrooms (to the original forty) and a laboratory at the north end of the structure.

4. P. Thornton Marye designed Daniel C. O'Keefe Junior High (1922-24), Pringle and Smith built Joseph E. Brown West Junior High (1923-24), and G. Lloyd Preacher designed Mary Lin Elementary (1928-30), Grant Park Elementary (1930), Whitefoord Elementary (1928-29), and additions to many others during the period.

5. Louie D. Newton, "Atlanta Will Have Another Skyscraper," *The City Builder* (October 1928): 17, 43.

6. In 1927-28, the First Baptist Church moved farther north along Peachtree Street to #745 and is currently abandoning that Midtown site to move north again to the suburbs.

7. The serpent was sacred to Asclepius, the legendary Greek physician, son of Apollo and Coronis, who became so skillful at healing that he could revive the dead, whereupon Zeus killed him. The single snake symbol of medicine, linked to Asclepius, has been largely replaced since the sixteenth century by the caduceus, a wing-topped staff with two snakes entwined around it. The caduceus was carried by Hermes, given to him by Apollo according to one legend, and has generally symbolized neutrality and noncombatant status, carried from ancient to modern times by Greek heralds, ambassadors, and postal service officials. Since 1902, it has been the official insignia of the medical branch of the U.S. Army.

8. The Davis-Fischer Sanatorium was founded by doctors E. C. Davis and L. C. Fischer and moved in 1911 to the new Linden Street location, just off Peachtree Street, following the completion of a new building there. Both the original structure and Wachendorff's 1923 addition were constructed of red brick with limestone trim and classical limestone porticos. In 1931, following the death of Dr. Davis, the privately owned sanatorium became the Crawford W. Long Memorial Hospital, named for the Georgia physician who first used ether during surgery. Crawford Long Hospital was initially supported by charity but in 1939 was deeded as a gift to Emory University, becoming part of what would become the famous Emory University Medical Center. At Crawford Long, a 1938 connecting building by Hentz, Adler and Shutze had been completed just before the donation to Emory, and a classically detailed School of Nursing building (1940) would immediately follow, designed by the same firm. Philip Shutze added the Emily Winship Woodruff Maternity Center in 1944.

9. A 1916 zoning "setback" ordinance in New York required skyscrapers to step back from the initial wall plane at various heights

in order to allow sunlight to reach sidewalk and street amidst crowded and towering skyscrapers. The resulting setback profiles soon influenced skyscraper design outside New York.

10. South Miami Beach has the nation's richest ensemble of Art Deco era landmarks—small hotels, apartment buildings, and commercial structures comprising a historic district that has been rightfully enlarged in recent years as new research and a broader sensitivity disclose the significance of this extraordinary oceanside Mecca for Decophiles.

11. "'Long Distance' Has Magnificent Home in Atlanta," *The City Builder* (December 1930): 5.

12. Ibid., 7.

13. Ibid., 5-6.

14. Ibid., 7. Each month in 1928 an average of 94,457 calls originated in Atlanta (incoming averaged 104,753). Calls were up 15 percent from January 1929 to July 1, 1930, with an average of 4,250 originating (and 4,000 switched, that is, incoming) long-distance calls daily by the end of 1930.

15. Norman Shavin and Bruce Galphin, *Atlanta: Triumph of a People* (Atlanta: Capricorn Corporation, 1982), 160.

16. City Hall was constructed on the site of the John Neal home (1859-64), which served as the headquarters of General Sherman on September 8, October 3, and November 14-16, 1864.

17. Dudley Glass, "Will Atlanta Keep Growing? Look at Five Points," *The City Builder* (June 1930): 6.

18. The 1933 Louisiana State Capitol by Dreyfous and Seiferth in Baton Rouge offers an example of the influence of this new model. *See* Vincent F. Kubly, *The Louisiana Capitol: Its Art and Architecture* (Gretna, La: Pelican Publishing Co., 1977) and Ellen Roy Jolly and James Calhoun, *The Pelican Guide to the Louisiana Capitol* (Gretna, La.: Pelican Publishing Co., 1980).

19. *The City Builder* (June 1925): 49.

20. Carson Pease, "Atlanta's Magnificent Old City Hall" (author's collection: unpublished manuscript, March 19, 1985), 3. *See also* Julian Wade Adams, "G. Lloyd Preacher, Southern Architect: A Study of His Career" (master of historic preservation thesis, University of Georgia, 1987).

21. Bletter and Robinson, *The Skyscraper Style.*

22. Druid Hills was a late design of noted landscape architect and community planner Frederick Law Olmsted, designer of Central Park in New York. Olmsted was invited to Atlanta from Biltmore Estate (Asheville, North Carolina), where he was at work for the Vanderbilts in their new chateau of the 1890s, to design a master plan for Druid Hills. Olmsted's scheme became the basis of the development of Druid Hills after 1908, with extensive construction of houses in the 1920s, including a luxury apartment hotel at the entry to Druid Hills, The Briarcliff ("Ten-Fifty Apartments"), designed in 1925 by G. Lloyd Preacher, who, by the way, lived in Druid Hills.

23. During the ten-year period from 1916 to 1925, the following Ponce de Leon apartment buildings had been constructed: The Kenilworth/Ivanhoe Apartments (1916), The Rosslyn (by Leila Ross Wilburn, 1916), The Ponceanna (1917), The Wyoming Apartments (1919-20), The Grove Park (ca. 1920), The One Ninety Apartments (by G. Lloyd Preacher, 1921), The Grandeleon (1922), The Druid Court Apartments (by Alexander F. N. Everett, 1922), The Bonaventure Arms (later Clairmont Hotel) (1923), The Massellton (by Emil C. Seiz, 1924), The St. Augustine Apartments (1924), #856 Ponce de Leon (1925), and The Ponce de Leon Apartments (1925). Other newly built apartments were located on the nearby streets of St. Charles Avenue and Frederica Street.

24. This character is evidenced in surviving automobile streets from Detroit to Birmingham, Alabama, and other metropolitan sites

nationwide. In the 400 block of Peachtree Street in Atlanta, the facades of the United Motors Service Building and the Peasant Building give indication of a short stretch of one of Atlanta's earliest automobile streets.

25. Atlanta Urban Design Commission, *Atlanta's Lasting Landmarks* (Atlanta: Atlanta Urban Design Commission, 1987), 29.

26. Bernice L. Thomas, "Five & Dime Design: The Legacy of Dime-Store Magnate Samuel H. Kress Lives on in Downtowns From Coast to Coast," *Historic Preservation* 45, no. 1 (January/February 1993): 62-70.

27. The hybrid Deco houses of Miami Beach during the period synthesized Art Deco ornament, Streamlined Moderne forms, and Modern planarity, ribbon windows, and flowing volumetric spaces in distinctive local examples of Deco-era residential design. New York houses by Edward Durell Stone and Los Angeles area houses by Richard Neutra and Rudolf Schindler were precociously Modern during the late 1920s and 1930s, reflecting earlier than anywhere in the United States the Bauhaus-inspired International Style Modern whose reflection in Atlanta is discussed in the following volume.

28. For a discussion of Evans' take-over of authority from William Joseph Simmons as Imperial Wizard of the Ku Klux Klan, see Charlton Moseley, "William Joseph Simmons," *Atlanta History: A Journal of Georgia and the South* 37, no. 1 (Spring 1993): 17-32.

29. Francis Neville Everett, son of the architect, described the Art Deco detailing in these terms. Atlanta Urban Design Commission, *Atlanta's Lasting Landmarks*, 63.

30. John Clark McCall, Jr., "The Grand," De-Give Opera House File, Atlanta Historical Society Archives, no pagination.

31. Thomas Lamb's 1936 Lake Theater in Oak Park, Illinois, was a period Deco work fully independent of Lamb's earlier historicist styles.

32. "Moderne" was a term used by contemporaries in the Deco-to-Modern era to describe the phase of modernism we here call Art Deco. "Art Deco" is the term more frequently adopted for the style by writers from the 1960s on. The distinction herein made between Art Deco and Streamlined Moderne design was not reflected in the 1920s/1930s general use of the term "Moderne" for the period's progressive design.

33. Information on the Lamb remodeling of the DeGive Opera House is from McCall, "The Grand."

34. Dudley Glass, "Peachtree—The Broadway of the South," *The City Builder* (December 1926): 49.

35. Today, the Ritz Carlton Hotel occupies the site.

36. In addition to the Art Deco theaters discussed, Atlanta neighborhood theaters of the period included 1) the Madison Theater, East Atlanta, 1927; 2) the Capri Theater, Buckhead, 1928-29; 3) the Temple Theater, Grant Park, 1934; 4) the Hilan Theater, Virginia Highlands, 1935; 5) the Garden Hills Theater, Garden Hills, 1940; and 6) the Gordon Theater, West End, 1946.

37. Thomas Morgan was a founder in 1906 of the Atlanta Chapter of the American Institute of Architects. His partner Alexander C. Bruce was the first national AIA member (an associate member since 1873 when he practiced in Tennessee) to practice in Atlanta, and the Bruce and Morgan partnership in Atlanta dates from 1882-1904. John Robert Dillon became associated with the Bruce and Morgan firm in 1903, and following Bruce's retirement in 1904, the firm of Morgan and Dillon continued until 1919 when Edward S. Lewis became a partner in Morgan, Dillon, and Lewis. The firm's work in the Fairlie-Poplar District includes the Grant-Prudential Building (1898, Bruce and Morgan), the Empire Building (1901, Bruce and Morgan), the Georgia Railway and Power Building (1904-7, Morgan and Dillon), and the Healey Building (1913, Morgan and Dillon with W. T. Downing, associate architect).

38. Jodi Iseman, "Downtown Atlanta's Commercial and Institutional Buildings of the 1920s and 1930s" (author's collection: unpublished manuscript, 1985), 25-26.

CHAPTER 3

1. Mary Huff, ed., *The Fabulous Fox: The Magic and the Memories* (Marietta, Ga.: Publications Concepts, Inc., 1990), no pagination [4].

2. Examples include: Mayan Revival Style: Mayan Theater, Los Angeles (Morgan, Walls, and Clements, 1927, 1,491 seats), Mayan Theater, Denver (Montana Fallis, 1930, 966 seats), the Fisher Theater, Detroit (Mayger and Graven, 1928, 2,975 seats), and the Aztec Theater, San Antonio (R. B. Kelley with Meyer and Holler, 1926, 3,000 seats); Chinese: Grauman's Chinese Theater, Hollywood (Meyer and Holler, 1927, 1,800 seats); Spanish Colonial and Mission: the Fox-Arlington Theatre, Santa Barbara, California (Plunkett and Edwards, 1931, 1,825 seats); Spanish Renaissance or Mediterranean: Tampa Theater, Tampa, Florida (John Eberson, 1926, 1,500 seats) and the Majestic, San Antonio (John Eberson, 1929, 3,700 seats); Baroque Revivals: Ambassador Theater, St. Louis (Rapp and Rapp, 1929, 3,000 seats) and St. Louis Theater, St. Louis (Rapp and Rapp, 1926, 3,861 seats, now Powell Symphony Hall); and finally, Apache/ Navaho: the KiMo Theater, Albuquerque, New Mexico (Boller and Boller, 1927, 1,300 seats). For a history of movie theaters in the United States, *see* David Naylor, *American Picture Palaces: The Architecture of Fantasy* (New York: Prentice Hall, 1991). Atlanta had a small neighborhood theater in a Moorish style when the Madison Theater opened on Flat Shoals Road, East Atlanta, in 1927. An exotic Capri Theater was built in Buckhead in 1928-29.

3. Huff, *The Fabulous Fox* [8].

4. Carrère and Hastings' Spanish/Moorish Ponce de Leon Hotel and El Alcazar in St. Augustine, Florida date from 1888.

5. "Dr. John Wesley Kelchner's Restoration of King Solomon's Temple and Citadel, Helmle & Corbett, Architects," *Pencil Points* 6 (November 1925): 69-86.

6. David Gebhard and Robert Winter, *A Guide to the Architecture of Southern California* (Los Angeles: Los Angeles County Museum of Art, 1965), 64 and 80. In 1943, in this tradition, Atlanta would construct the Spanish Baroque-Revival Abbey Mausoleum at Westview Cemetery.

7. Huff, *The Fabulous Fox* [8].

8. Ibid. [14]. Architect Thomas H. Morgan, in a brief history of the Georgia Chapter of the AIA published in 1943, described an exhibit held in January 1927 at the High Museum of Art in Atlanta "of the designs submitted in the recent competition for the Yaarab Temple," but Morgan names only five firms: Hentz, Reid, and Adler; Marye, Alger, and Vinour; A. Ten Eyck Brown; Pringle and Smith; and G. Lloyd Preacher. In what must have been an understatement of populist appeal, he noted that after a private showing for Atlanta area architects, the exhibit "proved to be of real interest to the general public." Thomas H. Morgan, "The Georgia Chapter of the American Institute of Architects," *The Atlanta Historical Bulletin* 7, no. 28 (September 1943): 114.

9. The Fox design was essentially the work of project designer Ollivier J. Vinour. P. Thornton Marye, born in Virginia, had arrived in Atlanta in 1903 and built his first major work, Atlanta's Terminal Station, in 1903-4. Marye's Atlanta works include St. Luke's Episcopal Church (1906); the Walton Building (1910); the New North Exchange Building for Southern Bell (1916, razed); two noteworthy residences, the Roman Doric Gentry-McClinton House (1913) and the Georgian Revival Hollins Randolph House (1924); and Daniel C. O'Keefe Junior High (1922-24).

10. C. Howard Crane designed the Detroit, Brooklyn, and St. Louis Fox theaters, and Thomas W. Lamb designed the San Francisco Fox. According to David Naylor, the seating capacities were as follows: Detroit,

5,048; Brooklyn, 4,088; San Francisco, 4,651; St. Louis, 5,042. Naylor gives the Atlanta Fox capacity at 3,934, although this does not represent the original seating but subsequent and larger replacement theater seats, which reduced the orchestra capacity. *The Atlanta Journal* indicated that 4,504 persons attended the first show on Christmas Day in 1929, and this more accurately places the theater's capacity in its proper relationship to the other Fox theaters.

11. The Moller organ provided music for sing-alongs and preludes and occasional intermission concerts for twenty-five years until 1954, when its lack of maintenance forced its retirement. In 1963 the American Theater Organ Society and Joe Patten (later the Fox technical director) employed seven miles of electrical wiring, new leather and parts, and a rebuilt generator to renovate the mighty instrument. The "Mighty" Moller organ, originally purchased for $42,000, was valued in 1974 at $400,000.

12. "Fox Theatre in Shrine Mosque a 'Show Place': Every Visitor to the City Is Taken to the Fox, as a Matter of Course—Even the Theater Is a 'Show' Without Regard to the Picture or Stage Production," *The City Builder* (April 1930): 9.

13. Information on the Christmas Day events at the Fox Theatre was drawn from Ernest Rogers, "Gala Fox Opening Thrills Atlanta With Great Show: Trying First Performance Goes Off Flawlessly at Mosque Theater," *The Atlanta Journal*, December 26, 1929, reprinted in Huff, *The Fabulous Fox* [6].

14. *See,* for example, the discussion of Atlanta architect Philip Shutze's academic training and use of measured drawings, photographs of historic buildings, and scrapbooks in Elizabeth M. Dowling, "Philip Trammell Shutze: A Study of the Influence of Academic Discipline on His Early Residential Design," *The Atlanta Historical Journal* 30, no. 2 (Summer 1986): 33-54, and in Elizabeth M. Dowling, *American Classicist: The Architecture of Philip Trammell Shutze* (New York: Rizzoli, 1989).

15. *See,* for instance, William Brockedon,

Egypt and Nubia: From Drawings Made on the Spot by David Roberts, 3 vols. (London: F. G. Moon, 1846-49).

16. Huff, *The Fabulous Fox* [19-20].

17. "Fox Theatre . . . a 'Show Place,'" 9.

18. Huff, *The Fabulous* Fox [9].

19. The Loew's Grand had been remodeled by Thomas Lamb in the Art Deco style in 1932, dramatically altering the interior of the 1893 Grand Opera House. The fiftieth anniversary of the *Gone with the Wind* gala was held at the Fox in 1989; by that time, the Loew's Grand had been demolished following a fire.

20. In the 1970s this was upgraded to present 70-mm and 35-mm Dolby-sound films.

21. In 1983 Atlanta Landmarks and Joe Patten were honored by the Atlanta Urban Design Commission with Awards of Excellence in recognition of their work in saving the Fox.

22. The Fox was classed in the 3,000- to 5,000-seat category.

23. Huff, *The Fabulous Fox* [10-11].

CHAPTER 4

1. Martin Greif in *Depression Modern* does not distinguish formally the Modern Classic from general "Depression Modern" of the 1930s. Depression Modern describes an architectural period marked by a modern economy of form, line, and surface as reflective of the constraints of depression years in buildings of varying stylistic character. In earlier writings, my references to "WPA Classic" sought to link the restrained, yet official, classicism of government buildings (post offices, war memorials, courthouses, federal office buildings, etc.) of the 1930s especially to New Deal projects, although the style emerges before Roosevelt's "Hundred Days" agencies, and was certainly not restricted to buildings constructed by or financed by either the Works Progress Administration or the Public Works Administration. Art Deco historian Eva Weber calls the style "classical moderne" and associates it especially with New Deal

construction. I am particularly grateful to Jay C. Henry for his observations in distinguishing the Modern Classic and for allowing me to peruse chapters, before publication, of his *Architecture in Texas, 1895-1945* (Austin: University of Texas Press, 1993) containing a discussion of buildings of this period in the Lone Star State.

2. This section of Pryor Street was renamed Park Place after the building was sold by the Thornton family in 1981, and the Thornton Building today is known as the Ten Park Place Building.

3. "Work Begun on Atlanta's New $3,000,000 Post Office," *The City Builder* (May 1931): 4.

4. Ibid.

5. Eva Weber, *Art Deco in America* (New York: Exeter Books, 1985), 12.

6. Carol Flores, "The Early Work of Burge and Stevens, Stevens and Wilkinson, 1919-1949" (master of science thesis, Georgia Institute of Technology, August 1990), 47.

7. The Palmer Building was razed to make way for the Standard Federal Savings and Loan Building (1975) by Toombs and Creighton.

8. Louie D. Newton, "Palmer Will Enlarge Glenn Building," *The City Builder* (March 1928): 14.

9. *The Federal Architect* was a magazine published by the Association of Federal Architects, an organization formed in 1927 by the architects and planners of federal buildings in Washington, D.C.

10. "Can Modern Architecture be Good?" *The Federal Architect* (October 1930): 6, 8-9, quoted in *Washington Deco: Art Deco Design in the Nation's Capital*, Hans Wirz and Richard Striner (Washington, D.C.: Smithsonian Institution Press, 1984), 28.

11. William Robert Mitchell, Jr., *Lewis Edmund Crook, Jr., Architect (1898-1967): "A Twentieth-Century Traditionalist in the Deep South"* (Atlanta: The History Business, 1984), vi.

12. The north and west blocks were razed, although the south block (containing the

now closed Rhodes Theater), at the time of this writing, remains standing.

13. Rhodes Hall is the state headquarters of the Georgia Trust for Historic Preservation, which ironically could only look out its windows and watch the demolition of the significant commercial blocks to the north and west of the house. The surviving south block of Rhodes Center, abandoned and boarded up, was unable to offer a skyscraper site inasmuch as an elevated access ramp to Interstate 85 flies overhead.

14. See the following volume for a discussion of Briarcliff Plaza (1939). Rhodes Center's demolition may result in part from this fatal flaw of lacking extensive off-street parking, which Briarcliff Plaza provided from the beginning.

15. William Mitchell has published the original design proposal for the Presbyterian Center in *Lewis Edmund Crook*, 86. The Presbyterian Center is now part of the Grady Hospital system.

16. Paul Cret, "Ten Years of Modernism," *The Federal Architect* (July 1933): 8, quoted in *Washington Deco*, Wirz and Striner, 97.

17. Paul Cret, "A Recent Aspect of an Old Conflict," *General Magazine and Historical Chronicle* 40, no. 4 (July 1938), quoted from *Paul Philippe Cret: Architect and Teacher*, Theo Ballou White (Philadelphia: Art Alliance Press, 1973), 84, in "The Architectural Development of Georgia Tech," Warren Drury (master of architecture thesis, Georgia Institute of Technology, 1984), 163.

18. Wirz and Striner, *Washington Deco*, 97.

19. Georgia Tech's first contact with Paul Cret was in 1921, when Cret, joined by Warren P. Laird and Francis P. Smith, provided a master plan for the campus.

20. Spencer V. Montgomery, "Our Armory," *The Christmas Bulletin* (later *The Nautilus*) (Atlanta: Georgia Tech NROTC, 1937), no pagination.

21. The Atlanta architecture and engineering firm Robert and Co., Inc. drew the first design for the gymnasium in September 1934.

Funding from the PWA became available in February 1936, and the Robert and Co. plans were reworked by Matt Jorgenson of the firm Bush-Brown and Gailey. See Drury, "Architectural Development," 172.

22. The Works Progress Administration (WPA) was created May 6, 1935, almost two years after the PWA, and was headed by Henry Hopkins. Intended specifically to provide useful employment for millions of victims of the Great Depression, the program provided jobs for 8.5 million people (at a cost of $11 billion) during its eight years in existence. The PWA, on the other hand, existed less than six years, from July 1933 to March 1939, and was essentially a funding agency. WPA construction projects, according to the final report of the agency, included more than 125,000 public buildings, 650,000 miles of roads, 75,000 bridges, 8,000 parks, and 800 airports, in addition to WPA's building or improving more than 2,500 hospitals, 5,900 school buildings, and almost 13,000 playgrounds. As well known is the agency's funding of theater, arts, and writers' projects, including the famed WPA state guides. *Final Report of the WPA, 1935-1943* (Washington, D.C.: United States Government Printing Office, 1944), 27-29. The agency's name was changed to the Works Projects Administration in 1939.

23. Drury, "Architectural Development," 172-73. *See also* C. W. Short and R. Stanley-Brown, *Public Buildings: Architecture Under the Public Works Administration 1933-1939, Vol. 1* (New York: Da Capo Press, 1986), 320. Originally published (first half of) *Public Buildings: A Survey of Architecture of Projects Constructed by Federal and Other Governmental Bodies Between the Years 1933 and 1939 with the Assistance of the Public Works Administration* (Washington, D.C.: General Printing Office, 1939). As this book went to press, and ironically on the building's sixtieth anniversary, Georgia Tech demolished the Heisman Gymnasium and Auditorium, apparently unaware that the university was destroying one of the most notable New Deal streetscapes in the state.

24. I am grateful to David Savini for infor-mation on Georgia Tech's PWA and WPA projects.

25. Harold L. Ickes, "Public Works in the New Deal," *The Architectural Forum* 59 (September 1933): 151.

26. Harold L. Ickes, *Back to Work: The Story of PWA* (New York: Macmillan Company, 1935), 197, quoted in "The Intentions and Innovations of Techwood Homes: The First Federally-Funded Slum Clearance and Public Housing Project in the United States," Carol Flores (author's collection: unpublished manuscript, June 1992), 1.

27. Flores, "Techwood," 7.

28. Flores has noted, "During the late nineteenth and early twentieth century, European philanthropists, industrialists, and governments built housing and communities aimed at improving health, welfare, and productivity of low- and middle-income workers. Although some local projects were attempted, the United States remained the only developed country in the Western world without a national legislative and financial commitment to housing." "Techwood," 1.

29. It was built following the clearance of two of the worst slums in the city, Techwood Flats (or Tanyard Bottom) and a depressed black area between the campuses of Spellman and Morris Brown colleges.

30. Flores, "Techwood," 8-11.

31. Ibid., 13.

32. Ibid., 14-15.

33. Charles F. Palmer, "Atlanta—Yours and Mine," radio address on WGST on January 9, 1937 and Martin Pawley, *Architecture versus Housing* (New York: Praeger Publishers, 1971), 42-43, referenced in "Techwood," Flores, 19-20.

34. Richard Guy Wilson, introduction in *Public Buildings*, Short and Stanley-Brown, vii. (Hereafter: Wilson, *Public Buildings*, with page.) The Procurement Division of the Treasury Department was responsible for federal buildings.

35. Ibid.

36. "PWA Has Changed Face of U.S.," *Life* 8, no. 14 (April 1, 1940): 62, quoted in Wilson, *Public Buildings*, viii.

37. See note 1 above.

38. Wilson notes that WPA art does exist, but it is not the murals in federal post offices and courthouses. Wilson, *Public Buildings*, vii.

39. The Rohland mural from the Decatur Post Office is on the nineteenth floor of the Russell Building in Atlanta; the Ruellan mural from Lawrenceville was moved to the Russell Building and subsequently installed in the Federal Building in Athens, Georgia. For other post office art in Georgia, see "New Deal Art in Georgia: A Guide to Post Office Murals and Sculpture," pamphlet published by the Georgia Museum of Art, University of Georgia, Athens, Georgia, 1990. For information on post office art of the New Deal nationally, see Sue Bridwell Beckham, *Depression Post Office Murals and Southern Culture: A Gentle Reconstruction* (Baton Rouge and London: Louisiana State University Press, 1989); Marlene Park and Gerald E. Markowitz, *Democratic Vistas: Post Offices and Public Art in the New Deal* (Philadelphia: Temple University Press, 1984); and Karal Ann Marling, *Wall-to-Wall America: A Cultural History of Post Office Murals in the Great Depression* (Minneapolis: University of Minnesota Press, 1982).

40. Ibid., ii. In reviewing the PWA program, C. W. Short (of the PWA) and R. Stanley-Brown (of the Treasury Department's Building Division) noted, "The greatest architectural advance has been made in the designing of utilitarian buildings, such as those connected with sewage and garbage disposal plants and water supply systems, which in former times were invariably ugly but which in many cases in the past 6 years have become structures of great aesthetic merit." In a short list of PWA projects nationally, the authors cite as "worthy of special note" the state prison at Atlanta, no doubt referring to the Tattnall Prison (Tucker and Howell, 1936) near Reidsville, Georgia.

41. Wilson, *Public Buildings*, x.

42. *America Builds: The Record of the PWA* (Washington, D.C.: United States Government Printing Office, 1939), 103-4, 129-30. The Atlanta schools included over twenty high schools and elementary schools. Only three were new schools constructed entirely by the New Deal agencies: 1) E. L. Connally Elementary School by Jesse Wilhoit, 1936-37, WPA project (Wilhoit and Smith added three classrooms, an auditorium, and cafeteria in 1947-48 and six additional classrooms in 1955-56); 2) Garden Hills Elementary by Tucker and Howell, 1938, WPA project (an auditorium and cafeteria were added in 1949—architect not known but probably Tucker and Howell, who designed a 1957-58 addition to the school as well); 3) Haygood Elementary School (now Atlanta Union Mission for Women) by Ivey and Crook, 1938, WPA project (the Auditorium addition is by H. Griffith Edwards, 1949-50, who would later enter into a partnership with John C. Portman, Jr.). The following represents New Deal improvements to older Atlanta schools, with the date and architect following the school indicating its original construction date and designer; in many cases pre- and post-New Deal additions were also made to these schools.

HIGH SCHOOLS:

A) Henry W. Grady High School (1923-24 Boys' High School, Hentz, Reid, and Adler): Print Shop, 1934-35, by Hentz, Adler and Shutze (CWA); Auditorium and Gymnasium, 1937-38, by Hentz, Adler and Shutze (WPA);

B) Franklin Delano Roosevelt High School (1922-24 Girls' Senior High School, Edwards and Sayward): Boiler House and Cafeteria, 1937, by Edwards and Sayward (WPA);

C) Booker T. Washington High School (1922-24, Eugene C. Wachendorff): Six classrooms and two laboratories addition, 1937-38, by Eugene C. Wachendorff (WPA);

D) Commercial High School: Classroom and library, 1934 (CWA).

ELEMENTARY SCHOOLS:

A) George Adair Elementary School (1912,

Edward E. Dougherty, now Area I Offices): Classroom addition, 1937, by Tucker and Howell (WPA);

B) Mary McLeod Bethune Elementary School (1928, Davis Street School, G. Lloyd Preacher): Auditorium, 1937, by Otis C. Poundstone (WPA);

C) H. R. Butler Elementary School (1912, original architect unknown, burned and razed, 1985): Addition, 1940 (WPA);

D) Capitol Avenue Elementary School (1922-24, Haralson Bleckley, now Continental Wingate of Georgia Home for Elderly): Auditorium, 1937, by Haralson Bleckley (WPA);

E) E. R. Carter Elementary (1911, Ashby Street School, rebuilt G. Lloyd Preacher, 1928): Four classrooms addition, 1935, by J. E. Wells (WPA);

F) Cooper Street Elementary (1922-23, Formwalt Elementary, DeFord Smith, now Atlanta Public Schools Environmental Services): Auditorium (ground-floor remodeling), 1935, by J. E. Wells (WPA);

G) East Lake Elementary School (built as courthouse, original date and architect unknown): Addition (probably auditorium), 1936-37, James C. Wise (WPA);

H) John B. Gordon School (1909-10, East Atlanta School, Battle and Barili): Addition, 1934 (CWA);

I) Home Park Elementary School (1910-11, Edward E. Dougherty, now State Street Academy Apartments): Five classrooms and cafeteria, 1937-38, by E. F. Billie (WPA);

J) David T. Howard Elementary School (1923-24, Arthur Neal Robinson, now Downtown Learning Center): East wing, 1937-38, by Arthur Neal Robinson (WPA);

K) C. D. Hubert Elementary School (1923-24, Atlanta Norman Training and Faith Elementary School, William J. J. Chase): Auditorium, 1937, by William J. J. Chase (WPA);

L) Samuel M. Inman Elementary (now Middle) School (1922-23, Virginia Avenue School, Warren C. Powell): Classrooms and library addition, 1937-38, by Warren C. Pow-ell (WPA); the auditorium had earlier been added (to Powell's original design) by G. Lloyd Preacher in 1929;

M) Jerome Jones Elementary School (1928-30, G. Lloyd Preacher, burned and razed, 1986): Classrooms, cafeteria, library, and "general repairs," 1934, architect unknown (CWA);

N) Morningside Elementary (1928-30, architect unknown): Auditorium, 1934, by George Harwell Bond with CWA assistance to Building and Grounds Committee;

O) Tenth Street School: Auditorium and classrooms, 1934 (CWA);

P) Whitefoord Elementary School (1928-29, G. Lloyd Preacher): Four classrooms, 1933-34 (CWA and FERA project).

The above summary is derived from archival material at the Atlanta Board of Education Facilities Division and from Gilbert H. Boggs, Jr., ed., "A History of the Georgia Civil Works Administration, 1933-34," the latter document prepared under the direction of Gay B. Shepperson, Federal Emergency Relief Administrator in Atlanta, and included in the appendix of "New Deal for Better Education," Wendy Taylor (author's collection: unpublished manuscript, 1991).

43. Tom Wolfe's *From Bauhaus to Our House* describes the impact of German Modernism on American architecture and culture. For a personal discussion by an Atlanta architect of the shift from Beaux-Arts (Classical) to Bauhaus (Modern) influences see Harold Bush-Brown, *Beaux Arts to Bauhaus and Beyond* (New York: Whitney Library of Design, 1976). For a discussion of the gradual transformation of architectural education in Atlanta from Beaux-Arts to Bauhaus, see Elaine Luxemburger, "The Transition from the Beaux Arts Tradition to the Bauhaus Influence in American Architectural Education" (master of science thesis, Georgia Institute of Technology, 1986). The Bauhaus was founded in Weimar, Germany, in 1919, moved to Dessau, Germany, in 1925, and finally moved to Berlin in the 1930s, where it

was closed by the Nazis. Many of its faculty, including its founder and first director, Walter Gropius, fled Germany to other countries in Europe and eventually emigrated to the United States. In the late 1930s, Gropius became head of the Graduate School of Design at Harvard; his student, Marcel Breuer, joined him there; Ludwig Mies van der Rohe became director of the Armour Institute (later Illinois Institute of Technology) in Chicago; and Lazlo Maholy Nagy established the New Bauhaus in Chicago. The influence of the earlier Ecole des Beaux-Arts in Paris, founded on historical traditions of classical art and architecture, was soon displaced in American schools of architecture with consequent results evidenced in the progressive Modern forms of American architecture, especially after World War II.

Selected Bibliography

Atlanta. Atlanta: The Women's Chamber of the Commerce, 1939.

Atlanta Urban Design Commission. *Atlanta's Lasting Landmarks.* Atlanta: Atlanta Urban Design Commission, 1987.

Battersby, Martin. *The Decorative Twenties.* Revised and edited by Philippe Garner. 2d ed. London: The Herbert Press, 1976.

Bayer, Patricia. *Art Deco Architecture: Design, Decoration, and Detail from the Twenties and Thirties.* New York: Harry Abrams, Inc., Publishers, 1992.

———. *Art Deco Source Book.* Secaucus, N.J.: Quartro Publishing, 1988.

Bletter, Rosemarie Haag and Cervin Robinson. *The Skyscraper Style.* New York: Oxford University Press, 1975.

Bossom, Alfred. *Building to the Skies: The Romance of the Skyscraper.* London: The Studio Ltd., 1934.

Bush-Brown, Harold. *Beaux Arts to Bauhaus and Beyond.* New York: Whitney Library of Design, 1976.

Capitman, Barbara Baer. *Deco Delights: The Beauty and Joy of Miami Beach Architecture.* New York: E. P. Dutton, 1988.

Cheney, Sheldon. *The New World Architecture.* New York: Tudor Publications, 1930.

The City Builder. Atlanta: Chamber of Commerce, 1916 through 1935 (most issues at the Atlanta History Center Archives).

Drury, Warren. "The Architectural Development of Georgia Tech." Master of architecture thesis, Georgia Institute of Technology, 1984.

Duncan, Alastair. *American Art Deco.* London and New York: Harry Abrams, Inc., Publishers, 1986.

———. *Art Deco.* London: Thames Hudson, 1988.

Esherick, Joseph. "Architectural Education in the Thirties and Seventies: A Personal View." In *The Architect: Chapters in the History of the Profession,* edited by Spiro Kostof. New York: Oxford University Press, 1977.

Ferriss, Hugh. *The Metropolis of Tomorrow.* New York: Ives Washburn, 1929.

Fleming, Douglas Lee. "Atlanta, the Depression, and the New Deal." Ph.D. dissertation, Emory University, 1984.

Flores, Carol. "The Early Work of Burge and Stevens, Stevens and Wilkinson, 1919-1949." Master of science thesis, Georgia Institute of Technology, 1990.

Greif, Martin. *Depression Modern: The Thirties Style in America.* New York: Universe Books, 1975.

Hillier, Bevis. *Art Deco of the 20s and 30s.* London: Studio Vista, 1968.

———. *The World of Art Deco.* New York: New American Library-Dutton, 1971.

Horsham, Michael. *'20s and '30s Style.* Secaucus, N.J.: Book Sales, Inc., 1989.

Huff, Mary, ed. *The Fabulous Fox: The Magic and the Memories.* Marietta, Ga.: Publications Concepts, Inc., 1990.

Lyon, Elizabeth Anne Mack. "Business Buildings in Atlanta: A Study in Urban Growth and Form." Ph.D. dissertation, Emory University, 1971.

Mitchell, William Robert, Jr. *Lewis Edmund*

Crook, Jr., Architect (1898-1967): "A Twentieth-Century Traditionalist in the Deep South." Atlanta: The History Business, 1984.

Shavin, Norman and Bruce Galphin. *Atlanta: Triumph of a People.* Atlanta: Capricorn Corporation, 1982.

Short, C. W. and R. Stanley-Brown. *Public Buildings: Architecture Under the Public Works Administration 1933-39, Vol. 1.* Edited by Richard Guy Wilson. New York: Da Capo Press, 1986.

Stevens, Preston Standish. *Building a Firm: The Story of Stevens and Wilkinson Architects, Engineers, Planners, Inc.* Atlanta: privately printed, © 1980.

Thomas, Bernice L. "Five & Dime Design: The Legacy of Dime-Store Magnate Samuel H. Kress Lives on in Downtowns From Coast to Coast." *Historic Preservation* 45, no. 1 (January/February, 1993): 62-70.

Vieyra, Daniel I. *"Fill'er Up": An Architectural History of America's Gas Stations.* New York: Macmillan, 1979.

Vlack, Don. *Art Deco Architecture in New York, 1920-1940.* New York: Harper and Row, 1974.

Weber, Eva. *Art Deco in America.* New York: Exeter Books, 1985.

Wilson, Richard Guy. *The Machine Age in America, 1919-1941.* New York: Harry N. Abrams, Inc. and the Brooklyn Museum, 1986.

Wirz, Hans and Richard Striner. *Washington Deco: Art Deco Design in the Nation's Capital.* Washington, D.C.: Smithsonian Institution Press, 1984.

Index